Your Next Chapter

Five Steps to Creating the Life of Your Dreams

By Tina Meilleur

To my dear friend Debra —
to your fabulous next chapter
much love,
Tina

Copyright

Advance Praise

"For any woman who is looking to make a significant change in their life but has no idea where to start – this is the book for you. Tina expertly guides you from a place of stagnation to a place of happiness through an easy to follow process called CRAVE™. *Your Next Chapter* also offers online tools and workbooks, as well as a Facebook group which serves to make this process more interactive and motivational. If you want to be the author of your own next chapter, I recommend you start today by opening this book."
– Emily Dodart

"I found Tina's book at the perfect time, as I am currently embarking on my own Next Chapter! Tina's warm and engaging writing style drew me in, and her willingness to share insights from her own journey through this process have left me feeling inspired and confident I am on the right path for me! Thank you, Tina!"
– Lori Johnson

"The book is laid out in a very organized way to help you go through the steps of making life changes. It's helpful that the author has gone through the process in her own life and is able to give real world examples of how these steps worked for her. The examples in the book also helped me identify actions or excuses I may have been making in my own life that's prevented me from living to my full potential."

– *Tiffany Landry*

Dedication

To my dear husband Robert, who always saw my potential, even when I couldn't. He always encouraged me to go bigger and would say out loud what I could only dream about. He kept bringing up what he thought was possible for me, even though I would consistently dismiss such lofty aspirations. He has been my biggest supporter and my deepest love.

Robert taught me that I didn't have to settle for something less in my career, a marriage with less than a total commitment, or a life without adventure. And he has provided me with one of my greatest gifts, my stepson. For all of these things, I am grateful and proud to be his wife and life partner.

To my dear mom, who has always been a source of love, inspiration and support - I love you. You taught me how to be the woman I am and allowed me to believe I always had what it took to accomplish what I wanted. You showed me it was okay to be smart and funny and how I could combine career with home life. I love to giggle with you and just spend time being "us".

In memory of my sweet dad, who allowed me to be his "daddy's girl". He taught me strength and perseverance, kindness and love. He provided a magical childhood for us –the kind that he never got to enjoy - and for that, I am eternally grateful. I always feel his love and guidance from up above.

Table of Contents

Introduction

I'm Being Vulnerable and I Hope You Can Be Too

"Vulnerability is about sharing our feelings and our experiences with people who have earned the right to hear them."
Brené Brown

This book is a labor of love designed to offer you some help in an area of your life that is probably pretty important to you. You were drawn to this book, so my wish is that the guidance it provides will fill your heart with hope. I also think some of what follows may describe how you were feeling when you decided to pick up this book. My sincere hope is that you will learn to trust me and trust yourself as I unveil a process that I know can help you define your next life chapter and make it a reality. I've put my heart and soul into these words. It was difficult to tell my story in such a personal way. I had to get really vulnerable and it was scary, but I did that because I wanted you to know this is a safe place for you to let down your guard and be vulnerable as well. Only then will you be able to get in touch with how beautiful your next life chapter can be for you.

So bear with me while I venture to express some of what you may be feeling. I bet you are already very successful in your own right but still have some unanswered questions, right? You've done everything right so far. You've accomplished a lot. You've successfully navigated several phases of your life so far and have reached a pinnacle in your career. You're at the top of your game and could get to the next level – if that's what you wanted. But you're not sure. Sometimes you think you either want to hit the reset or the pause button and do a little checking in with yourself before you move forward.

You would love to take some time to figure it out, but you are so tightly scheduled you don't have any time for yourself. You've probably run your life efficiently but without building much time into the schedule for yourself. How many years have you spent taking care of others or supporting the success of a business that was not your own?

You want to know what is next for you, but you don't know where to begin. You know there is something more for you, something you are meant to do or to feel while fulfilling your life's work. You believe you are blessed with divine gifts and are meant to not only help others, but love yourself and your life as well.

You feel selfish for even thinking you deserve more out of life. So many people would give anything to have what you have. You feel blessed and lucky all at the same time, but you blinked and ten or even twenty years have passed. You are amazed at how much older you are – where did the time go? With each year of your continued success, the stakes get higher and higher for making the right "next move."

Your family and friends are wonderful, but even they don't know your deepest desires. Even if you shared your deep desires with them, you doubt they would understand. They might even think you were ungrateful. And even if they did understand, they can't offer the objectivity that would be so helpful to you.

I had some of the same questions you are now asking yourself. In my own life experience, I found the more I neglected myself, the more I began to disappear into the background. I didn't want to be in the spotlight because I felt I could no longer truly shine as myself. The more I wanted to hide my sadness and pain, the more I felt I was not fitting in – leaving me feeling like an outsider. I knew deep down that I had a lot to offer, it simply seemed like some others weren't willing to accept my gifts. This was disheartening, because my gifts are the most personal part of me and to reject those is to reject me. I felt misunderstood, but I felt I had no choice but to keep going.

There's a lot to my story, but it wasn't until I experienced a layoff from the company with which I had spent 18 years of my career that I began to take the time to reflect on what was next for me. When I got the news of the layoff and for a long time after, my emotions were all over the place. I was shocked, I cried, and I got angry. After many months, when I was finally able to step back, I realized I could learn a lot, draw from my past experience in reinventing myself, and I would be okay even if I allowed myself to be vulnerable.

I have made it out of the clouds into the bright sunshine and direction of my life today – this phase, this next life chapter – as it is meant to be. That is what I wish for you. I want you to have the clarity of purpose, the certainty of direction, and the vulnerability to accept the path you may not have fully envisioned, but is absolutely right for you. You will know it in your soul but your logical brain will tell you it's too good to be true. But you will feel it is right in your bones.

Your future might feel something like this. You will become your authentic self and you will finally feel comfortable in your own skin. You will let go of your guilt and decide to focus on yourself for a change. People around you notice a certain lightness about you – as if a weight has been lifted from your heart. You no longer feel as if you are doomed to a life of the same day after day. You will wake up with energy and look forward to each day. You will realize each new day is a new opportunity for you to live your best life. You will begin to experience the freedom that comes with putting yourself first. You will find you have even more energy for everyone else. You learn to say "yes" to the things that make the best use of your time and energy, and learn to say "no" to the things that should not be on your plate, but without the guilt you used to feel.

And, best of all, you allow your life to unfold beautifully because you have learned to trust yourself.

I won't promise you a rose garden. Getting to where you want to be can be difficult. My journey was difficult and sometimes painful. I want to share my journey and what I've learned to help you. I want to share my process with you along with my proven steps to help you navigate your very personal effort to reengage and reinvent. I want to offer you that safe place where you can stumble but remain committed to getting to where you want to go.

Have you tried to make meaningful change in your life before? I bet you have. I also bet things got in your way – not enough time, worrying about what others might think, or the effort became too difficult. When you run into any of these reasons, you tend to stop altogether. You react in a way that can be really damaging to your progress. You may decide the timing isn't right and you tell yourself you will get to it later, or, worse yet, you shut down altogether. I want to help you recognize these barriers that can pop up any time you attempt to do something really meaningful for yourself. I've been there and know these can be powerful deterrents that can steer you off course. But, I'll be here to show you how to break through these barriers and move forward in spite of them. Because you will be equipped to recognize your roadblocks and have the tools to deal with them, *this time, things can be different*!

I think it is very important to know your starting point when you begin such a life-changing effort. I promised you a safe place in which you could be vulnerable and explore. In the spirit of that promise, I have designed an assessment to help you see where you are right now in living your ideal life – to help you uncover your current state. This will be a great point of reference as you move through the process. It will not only help identify where you want to make changes, but in which areas change is most important for you and your happiness. This is a complimentary assessment and I urge you to take it now as you begin the book. You will also have an opportunity to take it again later after going through the process so you will be able to visualize your progress and celebrate.

So let's get started! Take a few minutes to complete the assessment to establish your baseline - you can find the assessment at this address: www.yourideallifequiz.com. After you take the assessment, you will receive your results pretty quickly. You can begin to get a picture of where you are doing well, and where you can begin to focus your efforts to create your ideal next life chapter.

Taking the assessment is your first step in this wonderful guided exploration of simple, yet effective steps to help you get what you want. This can truly become the best chapter in your life!

Chapter 1 – Acknowledge What Your Heart Knows

"Taking a break gives your heart and soul new life."
Tina Meilleur

I have plenty I want to share with you. My story may not be your story, but my hope is that some pieces of it may resonate with you and convince you that you are not alone in this quest for a meaningful next life chapter. I hope it will help you to step back and consider doing something important for you and your future – something that will fulfill you and help you achieve what *you* have been craving from your life – what your *heart* wants to feel.

At some point, I realized that life had a funny way of happening *to* me. I closed my eyes to the things I didn't want to see or acknowledge. I was letting things ride in a very passive way. It wasn't until I decided to take an active role in shaping my future for myself that things began to change. But much of this "shaping" had to do with not only the easy stuff – noticing when an opportunity presented itself – but also with the hard stuff – creating opportunities for myself. I learned it's what we do with opportunity that counts. We either find an opportunity or we create one – either way, it always involves *doing something*.

I had plenty of opportunities for reinventing my life. Some were opportunities I noticed and acted upon and others were thrust upon me. In any event, each one of them was a test, a challenge, to see if I could summon my inner strength and create a new version of myself.

My story is a history of personal reinventions that runs throughout my life. This history began at the end of high school, when I met the guy I thought was the love of my life. We were both eighteen and so in love. We really didn't have any clue about life outside our parents' homes, but that didn't stop us. I enrolled at the University as a freshman the fall after high school graduation, but was so distracted by the freedom that brought, I didn't take my courses that seriously and decided to drop out after one semester. We married that next year. I was so happy and in love.

Within a couple of years, at the age of 21, we bought our own home. It was brand new and a bit further away from the city, but it was wonderful. It was like being all grown up and living a dream. There was such excitement about being on our own, making our own way with such hopes for the future. Being with him was so consistent with the traditional vision of marriage that I saw growing up. He was in charge and I was clearly in the more traditional wife role. I had a full-time job, but he was the main breadwinner.

That bliss lasted about five years, at least for me. He had secured a job as a salesman at an auto dealership with a great deal of upside potential on commissions, so he had started to really enhance his earnings. I, on the other hand, was stuck in dead-end office jobs with no chance of promotion or salary growth. One weekend, he went on a "fishing" trip with the guys. He returned home on Sunday afternoon in a clean, pressed shirt and jeans, and smelling quite nice for someone who claimed to have been out in a fishing boat most of the weekend. Before I could even comment or ask questions, he said he was leaving me. My heart sank. I felt as if I had been kicked in the gut. I was in disbelief. I followed him outside as he got into his car and I was sobbing uncontrollably. He coldly instructed me to go back inside and allow him to leave.

I finally went inside, barely believing what had just happened. How could I have not seen this coming? What would I do now? How would I make ends meet? How could I live without him? My mind was swirling, my chest hurt from crying so uncontrollably, and my future felt like it had just imploded.

I had no real career, no education beyond high school, and no money. I was now a victim of my earlier choices – to quit college and get married. But I knew I was a fighter, a trait I had inherited from my father. He was in physical pain most of his life, but he still held a blue-collar job and worked extra shifts to make ends meet. I knew I had that in me as well.

We decided to rent the house since the real estate market was so depressed, and we each got an apartment. That turned out to be the first time I was out on my own, without my parents, and without my husband. Here I was at 24, finally independent and living on my own. Growing up in a way I hadn't experienced before.

After a while, we did begin to talk about what happened and he confessed to an extramarital affair. I had suspected this was the truth after he left, but I totally missed the signs before he left. Again, that was an area where I had closed my eyes to things I didn't want to see or acknowledge. After much soul-searching and some counseling, we gave our marriage another chance and got back together, but we eventually got divorced. It wasn't meant to be. I truly deserved better.

Now that I was single, I eventually got back into dating, I shared a beautiful rental home with two other single women, and finally decided to go back to college. At 28, I started over with my college education and made it a priority. I had lost the ability to concentrate on a more traditional college schedule and experience, so I had to work full-time and attend college whenever I could. I went at night, all day on Saturdays, every summer, and even negotiated with some of my more supportive bosses along the way to get those classes in during work hours that would have been impossible to get scheduled otherwise. My mantras became "No one can take my education away" and "I will never rely on anyone else again for my well-being." These were very powerful, because I realized I was doing this *for me*! Finally, I had come to terms with making myself a priority and being *bold* when I had to be in order to achieve my goal.

I went on to finally graduate with a B.S. in Accounting right before I turned 35. I was looking around every now and then for a position that might treat me as a new college graduate even at my age. Because I was older, I had great business experience. I had worked my way up to management positions in several smaller companies and had learned a great deal about managing businesses and profitability.

My opportunity finally came when I landed a position with a Fortune 500 company. I had just turned 40 and had recently passed the last sections for my CPA designation. Within a couple of years, I was in a director-level position, leveraging both my education and my extensive experience.

It was very gratifying to know that my hard work had finally paid dividends for my career.

In the meantime, my single phase lasted for about ten years, while I was trying to balance completion of my undergraduate degree and starting my new career. I dated some wonderful guys, but when I reflected on the disappointing ending of these relationships, I realized the only common denominator was me! I was drawn to men I thought I could "fix." The result was always the same: they would break up with me or I would find a fatal flaw that would not allow me to continue in the relationship. In one instance, I even got engaged. I was so excited, but as the engagement wore on, he shared that he wasn't sure he could be monogamous when we got married! I was floored! Needless to say, I gathered up my self-esteem and ended the relationship immediately. Again, I instinctively chose *me*!

I wrote off dating for a while and it was actually a welcome break. About the same time, my company nominated me for an Executive MBA program and I jumped at the chance. This was an opportunity to get an advanced degree and focus on something different. This program was also to be completed while working, so I was going to have a lot on my plate.

As I was nearing the last six months of the MBA program, I thought it would be nice to start focusing on my love life again. I thought it would be great if I could lay the groundwork for meeting some new men and to start dating when my schedule was more open. Prior to putting the word out to anyone, I did spend some time thinking about the type of man I would like to meet and what qualities and values were most important in a partner. At that time, I was 42 and didn't think I wanted to waste any more time with men who weren't a good fit for me. I knew I wanted a mix of loyalty, honesty, someone who shared my values for family and friendships, someone I could count on and who would love me for me. I had become a very strong, successful woman and didn't really need a man for financial support or to handle things for me, but that didn't mean it wouldn't be nice to have someone around that could take care of me from time to time and be a real partner in my life.

I met my husband-to-be and we began dating exclusively when I was finishing up my MBA program. Our program finished up in Paris with some international classes and I stayed an extra week with a friend in the program. She and I went sightseeing, shopping, and had a great time. While I was in Paris, he sent roses and a letter written in French to my hotel. When I returned from my trip, he picked me up from the airport with a surprise of chocolate-covered strawberries and champagne. Now this was someone worth getting to know a lot better!

We dated a while before he eventually introduced me to his adorable five-year-old son. We had dates as a couple and also eventually included his son as well. Over the next year or so, we gradually felt it was right to take our relationship to the next level and we got married in 2000. As I am writing this, we are celebrating our 15th wedding anniversary today.

During those years, my corporate career continued to be wonderful and motivating as I took on one challenging role after another. I was always viewed as a change agent, or the person who could go into an area to create something new, or clean up an area that needed some attention. I was always charged with a pretty large staff and spent a great deal of my time on coaching, mentoring, and professional development. I also felt an obligation to position my people for consideration for promotions and additional responsibility. This was an integral part of my career and one that I always enjoyed immensely.

But even as all of those good things were going on, I knew there was also something wrong. I wasn't happy, I wasn't challenged, and I wasn't as motivated as I had been. I realized I wasn't fully utilizing my talents and my abilities. I knew there was something else for me, and I had this nagging feeling deep in my gut. I didn't know what it was and I didn't know how to identify it. I only knew there was something greater out there for me – some way I could have a bigger impact in the world. I kept plugging along, not sure what to do, but afraid to make a move that would jeopardize what I had worked so hard to accomplish. The money and stability of my career was hard to walk away from.

My last project with the company involved leading the human resources side of the largest reorganization effort and downsizing in the company's history. I was responsible for things such as the selection process, the severance packages, the treatment of the benefits upon exit, etc. There were high stakes in this work and lots of interaction with the most senior executives in the company. The work was relentless, with great attention to detail, all while attempting to calm the nerves of those working with me on the project.

At least I didn't have time to think about how unhappy I had become – I was working around the clock! I assumed I could defer my thought process about whether to stay or leave for another few years. I was convinced that after the project was complete, there should be plenty of challenging work in rebuilding the organization and I would again be challenged and motivated.

But as the new organizational chart began cascading down the chain of command, I was left without a position. My old position had been eliminated in the reorganization effort. I had no position to go back to. I didn't have to make a decision – they made it for me! Those same feelings I had when I was 24 and my first husband left me came flooding back: "What am I going to do? Where will the money come from?" and a whole host of other life-altering questions.

I took many deep breaths the day I was told of my fate. I went home, shared the news with my husband and cried a lot! The next day was Friday and I stayed in bed all day. I had a big pity party all by myself. I spent the weekend in a fog, but tried to get myself together to return to the office on Monday. Yes, I had to go back and face both those who shared my fate and the survivors alike. I wasn't sure I could get through it.

On Monday, I found a new strength that I hadn't known I had. It must have been buried somewhere deep in my soul, but it showed up for me that day. I had to tell my project team about my fate and ask them to stay engaged so we could finish our work. I was so proud of my interaction with them and their response and support. I began to realize this wasn't my first experience with having to reinvent myself and start over. I had strong evidence that I would not only survive, but thrive.

Once I had the team under control, I began to focus again on me and what I would do next. I immediately jumped into my old comfort zone – making a plan to get more education or another corporate job. I shared my plans with a dear friend over lunch. She looked me in the eye and asked me, "Are you sure that's what you need?" She had just asked me what I needed to be asking myself!

I began to follow my instincts and my heart and consider what I had to offer. There I was, a CPA with an MBA, extensive small and large business experience in a variety of high profile areas, experience interacting with the most senior level executives and business owners, great with process and change management, and a sought-after mentor for other successful professionals. And, remember, one of the most rewarding aspects of my career had been my activities in professional development, coaching, and mentoring of others on my staff and in groups where I was a member.

After much soul-searching, I finally decided that I would follow my heart and intuition and formally declare my desire to be a life and business coach. I had a ton of experience in this, but decided to get some more formal training to round out my skills and provide my future clients with the best experience I could offer.

It took me a while to own this new area of focus for my career. Even with what I knew about my experience and abilities, it was a painful process to own this new profession as my own. I went through a lot of self-doubt, a crisis of confidence, and confusion about who might actually hire me as their coach.

I thought I would be best prepared to help clients who were looking to reinvent themselves and design their next life chapter. But I had to ask myself how I had been successful in this area and how my success might translate and allow me to be of service in this area of coaching. I began to explore how I had accomplished everything so far in my life. I was pleasantly surprised to realize I always had a way of establishing goals and achieving them. However, over time, I had become far less proactive and a lot more passive. I tended to drift toward the obvious, the easy path, the thing I thought I "should" do. I'd become complacent. I was adrift in my own lifeboat, praying no high seas or storms might occur and cause overall disruption in my life. I was living safely – I was living without a passion.

Deep down, I *knew* there was something missing – something significant. I was always busy, *and* I got a lot done every day. It was often work that I tried to make meaningful but which needed others to participate in order to affect change. Their apathy became an excuse for me not getting to the work I was meant to do. One of the blocks I developed was the ability to create excuses – reasons why I could not move toward what I was meant to do.

I always wanted to make a difference by using my talents and ability to influence others in a positive way. When I created excuses, they kept me safe – or so I thought. It felt like those excuses kept me grounded in reality so I wouldn't be disappointed if something new I tried didn't work out. But what the excuses really did for me was strip me of my soul's calling, my confidence, and my ability to take a risk for something worthwhile.

I had to learn to break away from what was comfortable. I had become so disconnected that I couldn't even identify what I was feeling anymore. It was as if I had a dull ache in my abdomen, but no idea what was causing it. I ignored it because it was not an acute pain, but it still bothered me in my quietest moments. Those quiet moments were few and far between. I hardly allowed myself any time to listen to my innermost thoughts and feel my emotions. I probably had mastery of the quick emotions, like anger or a moment of happiness, but nothing deeper than that. I was so disconnected from my true self.

I had always been able to use my imagination when I was a little girl. My imagination was an escape to a world of possibilities, with nothing to block my dreams. The process of growing up built those blocks, those feelings of "I can't," those worries of "I should." I wanted to recapture the possibilities of my youth while taking full advantage of the wisdom of my life. How could that be possible without throwing everything away?

* * *

If you are looking for something more meaningful in your life for your next chapter, it's very important to recognize that *you are not alone*. When I was going through my most recent transformation, I felt very alone. I now realize that was not the case, but I didn't know how many other people like me were out there. So, for you, no matter what your age, you can begin to see your life in phases or cycles. The traditional linear life model of working and then retiring for leisure doesn't hold any longer. Evidence suggests you will go through several phases of work and levels of engagement in the workforce before you hit that leisure retirement threshold much later in life.

I realized I was not alone in my quest when I attended an event with mostly female entrepreneurs who were either starting out or were very early in their businesses. There were approximately 750 of us at this event. The attendees included women who ranged in age between 30 and 80. There was a lovely woman in attendance who I felt I should meet based on her energy and style. I finally met her and had the opportunity to talk and visit with her during the event. I found out she was 73 and just beginning her sales consulting business. She had enjoyed a great career in sales and was hugely successful. She figured out she could teach others how to sell effectively and help them get out of their own way. The more people I met there, the more I realized these were some individuals just like me – working to reinvent themselves and live the life of their dreams.

During that event, I clearly saw the difficulty we can have in recognizing our own true talents. I found out very quickly when speaking to other entrepreneurs that I had a wealth of knowledge and experience that could help them. I also recognized how much each of them had to offer in their own lives and businesses. I took for granted that others knew what I knew, but that was not the case. We all had different talents and styles that we brought to the table. So, during that event, I realized the best way I could be of service was to share what I knew and help others be successful. I couldn't help but get motivated by sharing my time with them.

Let's look at another story to illustrate that you are not alone. Valerie was a lovely woman who was over 50, well-educated, had great experience, and was a delightfully smart female executive. She was the main breadwinner for her family and readily accepted that role. She worked hard and was devoted to her family. She had been with her husband for over 20 years, had two beautiful children who were in their 20s, and seemed happy. Over a period of time, things in her relationship had deteriorated and her husband asked for a divorce. She was devastated and heartbroken. She didn't understand what she'd done wrong.

To those around her, she seemed to have it all. She had an executive level position with a large company and had several prestigious board positions. She interacted easily with her male counterparts and was respected by those in her industry. She was seen as a role model for many who knew her. However, when her marriage disintegrated, she began to deal with feelings of self-doubt, inadequacy, and not being good enough. Some of those feelings were the result of her internal interpretation of her husband's words and actions during their relationship.

Once she was free of the marriage, she spent a great deal of time getting in touch with what she truly wanted. It was a painful time, but she sat with the discomfort and the hurt for many months as she worked through her thoughts and fears. She emerged with a clarity of purpose, a certainty about her desires, and an intention to live her life for herself. She was still very close to her children, but she decided to put herself first.

About a year later, having been in that place of putting herself first, she stumbled upon a new love interest. She had shed her fears and rebuilt her confidence as her own person – an independent woman, who was ready for what life had in store for her. She spent time with this new man and they got to know each other at a wonderfully deep level. This was a level she probably didn't expect, but because she had done her work, she was so much more available for true, deep love.

They were in a long-distance relationship for a while and began to have those wonderful heart-to-heart talks about "what if" and "when" and decided that schedules and distance were not meant to hold them back. She had fulfilled all of her career dreams up to that point, and decided that love was more important in her life. She moved to the city where he and his children lived in order to forge a new family relationship together. They have plans to get married next year and she has never been happier.

I share this story because it is a beautiful example of someone giving in to putting themselves first and not worrying about what others might think. She probably received some comments like, "Are you sure?" and "What if it doesn't work out?" but she knew in her heart, her gut, and her intuition that this was the path for her.

* * *

With each story that I uncovered as I was writing this book, I began to see how my experience was similar to so many others. I was captivated by the instinctual methods we all followed when making such dramatic changes in our lives. Those methods were many of the same ones we used to accomplish things when we were younger, but we had drifted away from them. When we get too comfortable, have too much at stake, or are uncertain where to go next, we often struggle with how to even get started on our next journey.

You will see case studies like Valerie's throughout the book. I want you to really begin to feel you are not alone in your desires or your quest. I want you to give yourself permission if you want to make a difference, do something more meaningful, undertake something very important to you, or focus on something you have always wanted. I want to help you learn to give yourself that permission.

When I did set a goal and took action, I found that there was always something that caused me great discomfort and that would result in my second-guessing myself. I had gotten so used to not feeling any strong emotions that when they came up I became so distressed I simply wanted the pain to stop. I would quickly move on to the "next thing," leaving the emotion to be dealt with later.

This became a pattern of avoidance for me. I eventually realized I could not move forward with any big goals unless I could free myself of that avoidance pattern. I had to dig deep and get to the emotions that I had been pushing down for a long time.

* * *

I have a deep craving to share my message. I want to start a movement to help other successful people explore and dream about what to do for their next life chapter. So I asked myself how I could be of service to others in their quest. I knew I could help others because I had done the same thing for myself so many times in my life. You're probably like this, too – you probably know how you got to your most successful place. What I had figured out was how to reinvent myself for my next life chapter by leveraging what I knew and what I had to offer when the opportunity presented itself. I broke the code along the way to get beyond the self-doubt and understand that I could be successful in this next life chapter – to actually believe it and make it happen.

I chose to write this book to help those of you who are like me. You've been struggling with that nagging feeling of wanting more for yourself and not knowing where to start. I went through a real exploration process, one that wasn't without its messiness. I got through to the other side and I am so much happier. It wasn't always fun, but I was able to break it down and control the feelings of overwhelm and the self-doubt in a way that allowed me to keep moving forward. That was the blessing of having a process and a plan. Without it, I think I would have abandoned my desires and shut down like I have done so many times in the past. I want you to have that same blessing – to have a process and a plan – so you can work toward achieving your ideal next chapter.

I want to guide you through the excitement and the discomfort that may come up as you explore and define your own process and plan. I want to show you there is a way to move forward without shutting down and abandoning your dreams. All things are possible for you when you recognize what you have to offer and claim your brilliance and desires.

You are not alone. More than half of people over 40 want to actively reengage in their working life in a different way – a way that is more satisfying and that feels more balanced. It is all about how you think about your life. So many others feel the way you do.

So, how about you? Have you settled and abandoned the things that really matter in your life? When did you stop believing nothing else was possible for you? When did you decide your life had reached its pinnacle – that it was already the best it was ever going to be – and so you should just accept it? How did you get here? Why are you now waking up and noticing the situation?

What you desire doesn't have to turn your world upside down. I used the steps I am sharing with you in this book to reinvent myself for this chapter in my life. In the process, I also had to *reengage*. I had stepped back from almost anything that gave me joy – all in the name of the big three deterrents to my happiness: no time, no energy, and believing I wasn't deserving. What a powerful triad of excuses, don't you think? I had convinced myself those excuses were real. Even as they swirled around my brain, I had trouble believing they were powerful enough to stop me from taking action on things I really wanted to do. But they did.

I can prepare you for what's ahead and help you reengage and find joy again. I can help you to anticipate the reactions of those around you and deal with them effectively. When you start to make change, you aren't the only one who might feel a little uncomfortable. I remember a friend who is a recovering alcoholic. His wife married him when he was in the throes of his alcoholism. He sought help and when he got sober, his wife didn't like the person he became. When he was drinking, he was happy go lucky and wasn't paying attention to how she was spending their money. Once he got sober, he was more engaged in their life and finances, and she eventually left him. In his case, he had to make the changes he needed in his life, but she was not interested in hanging around. I realize there are always two sides to every story, so I'm not criticizing her, I'm simply pointing out how change can affect those around you. They begin to wonder how your changes will affect *them*. You can be aware of this impact on those you love and deal with this aspect of your change honestly and lovingly.

I can also help you recognize whether what you are experiencing is fear or a reaction to something that isn't right for you. When you begin to make change, you can start second-guessing yourself and begin to doubt your path. This is normal and there are ways to identify fear and bust through it so you can make real progress. Fear may be the reason you haven't been successful in the past in making a meaningful change in your life. But maybe what you're starting to do isn't right for you. In that case, this process will simply allow you to go back and make another choice!

I want you to see what is possible for you and I want to help you find confidence. I can do that by being your experienced guide on this journey. I won't abandon you during the tough times. I'll offer you tools and techniques to get through the exploration and planning so you can develop the courage to see your goals all the way through to completion.

I know how important it is to be prepared for what may happen and to be able to share how you are feeling. I remember having surgery and the surgeon shared information about what to expect when I went in for the procedure and during the healing process. That made my recovery so much easier. When something occurred, instead of being worried about what was happening to me, I was confident it was part of the process he had shared with me. I also remember being terribly anxious when I was wheeled into the surgery suite, but I remembered that the anesthesiologist had told me to let her know what I was feeling. When I did, she said she had just the "cocktail" I needed. Anxiety gone!

When someone can anticipate your questions, your anxiety, or your reluctance, it sends a powerful message you are in good hands. You can place your trust in those who have gone before you, have the experience to know what the issues are, and the skills to help you get through them. I want to be that guide for you. Place your trust in me and we can experience this together. The exploration itself can be so much fun and full of excitement.

Your next chapter can be the best so far, but certainly not your last. You will become a role model for your friends and family -

they will admire you for making it happen for yourself.

Here's to your next chapter – happy exploring!

Chapter 2 – Growing into All You Can Be

"You are most uncomfortable when you are ready for personal growth."
Tina Meilleur

Reinventing Yourself is Not New to You

You may not believe you have ever had the opportunity to reinvent yourself during your lifetime, or perhaps didn't recognize it when you did, but consider the following potential examples from different phases of your life.

When you were a small child, anything you tried that went wrong and got you into trouble resulted in a rather short recovery period. You were probably so cute your transgression was quickly forgotten. When you were in elementary school, you may have felt that you only had to get to eighth grade to get a new chance at reinventing yourself (perhaps the dream was only getting to middle school, right?) Then, in high school, you were changing and adapting to a totally different social construct and learning how to survive the perceptions and opinions of your peers. For you, that may have been both a wonderful and often painful time of getting comfortable in your own skin. You made it past high school and had yet another opportunity to reinvent yourself, this time in a much larger pool – college! That's where you really started to spread your wings and become your own person.

When you began working and establishing your career, you were full of excitement and promise and in an environment in which you could be pretty bold about your choices. You may have made a safe job choice, but hopefully you made that job the best it could be through your attitude, your contributions, and your energy.

If you decided to marry, or have children, got divorced, or now even have grandchildren, you have had many opportunities to change and adapt and reinvent yourself in your lifetime. You have had lots of chances to change the way you operate and perceive yourself and how you project yourself to others.

I hope you see you have had a lot of opportunities to change the way you perceive yourself and what you do and how others around you view who you are. Hopefully, by now, you have learned to recognize and appreciate your experience.

You've Been Conditioned to Be Successful but Play It Safe

Let's step back a minute to explore how you may have been socialized during your life. You were probably forced to compete in school for grades, attention, and with the opposite sex for your place in the world. This competition may not have been so obvious every day, but it was there. Layer your parents' and teachers' expectations on top of that, and you can see you had a lot of people to please. Women are socialized with other women in a certain way, just as men are socialized with other men in a certain way. While you are in school, peer pressure is at an all-time high. How you handle this pressure sets the tone for the rest of your life. Caring about what other people think and not being able to break free from that dynamic can set you up for a lot of challenges in your life.

For those who break free of the traditional expectations, they take on life with abandon, often making the choices others might consider risky. They are more likely people who take some time off after completing their degree to travel the world because they want to truly experience life before they settle down. Then there are others who never settle down – they enjoy the freedom they have in life and place importance on different priorities. Some live a life with no regrets. They are often the big risk takers whose actions lead to big payoffs or major disappointments – everything they do is "all or nothing." This type of life is not for the faint of heart, especially for those who desire a more traditional career and life structure.

For those who pursue a more traditional path, when they get that first big career break or make that first major life decision, they are on top of the world. They feel they can accomplish anything and the world is their oyster. They have a great education, a support system, great experience, and opportunities to do something really great with their life. This fuels their boldness to try new things within their career and in their life as long as these fit the more traditional definition of success.

How about you? You start with an idealized dream about how your life will play out and it usually gets you to the point of being successful in your career, being a great parent to your children, or both. Later, you begin to worry about rocking the boat – not wanting to jeopardize what you have worked hard to achieve so far. Rarely do you think beyond that point. You begin to make "playing it safe" a priority. You feel there will always be time to plan the "next thing."

Do You Still Have Time to Make a Difference?

"We cannot start over but we can begin now, and make a new ending."
Zig Ziglar

I'm sure you can think of a time in your past when things were going well and you were extremely happy. When did that happiness start to diminish? Can you pinpoint the exact time? Some people can pinpoint it because they experience it as a pivotal day in their life when everything changed. For others, it happens ever so gradually so they don't notice until it is right in front of them. It can feel as sudden as going to bed feeling fine and waking up with a piercing migraine. It's different for everyone, but the result is the same.

How has it been for you? Did you realize one day you were less happy, less satisfied, less motivated, and paid less attention to what you want than you ever did? Did you tell yourself there will be time to do all the things you want to do? That can be a big lie, because time to plan the "next thing" starts slipping away. You can blink and years have passed.

In a *Washington Post* article published recently and written by Sally Abrahms, she stated there are 75.4 million baby boomers in the United States. The baby boomers cover those from 51 to 69 years of age. There is also an AARP (formerly also known as the American Association of Retired Persons) study referenced in that same article that cites one in five workers between ages 45 and 74 had either taken leave or quit a job to care for an adult family member in the last five years. There is also a growing number of couples who are divorcing in their 50s and 60s, after their child-rearing is complete.

It's clear from this data that the age group from 45 to 65 and even up to 70 has lots of challenges, but this group is probably the best prepared for taking a leap before they feel it is too late for them. They often say, "If not now, when?" When is the right time to start taking time for yourself and doing what is right for you? The answer is *now*!

I listened to an interview with Kobe Bryant today in which he discussed when he knew it was time to quit playing basketball. He said he spends 15 minutes every morning in quiet thought, but his mind would always drift back to basketball. He noticed one day that his mind didn't bring him back to basketball during that quiet morning time. It happened again and again. That became his signal that it was "time," and he started thinking about what his next chapter might be. He then began to plan his announcement, taking into account his respect and admiration for his fans. We will hear more from him as he makes his plans for his next chapter and I can't wait to see what he has in store for himself and his fans.

For me, even as I grew disenchanted with my corporate career, one of the fallacies I bought into was my "lack of runway," as I called it. I told myself I didn't have enough time to do what I wanted to do or to be successful in another endeavor that was totally different from what I knew.

Even though it is true that as we age, we have less and less time to make the impact we want to make, it is also true that we can do anything we set our minds to. It's like exercising. We can always find an excuse to skip our exercise on any given day or week, but every day we do follow through absolutely counts.

So, let's get back to this "lack of runway" concept. With mortality ages rising and older citizens remaining productive well into their later years, we have a lot more "runway" left than we used to. Retirement is no longer the same concept it was for our grandparents or maybe even our parents. They would often work until they were 65 and then move into leisure retirement.

My best friend's parents are in their 90s, and her dad was an engineer for a major oil company for the majority of his career. He planned to retire in his 50s and did so at 58.

He had a strong economic plan for his family, but he also had a strong social one as well. He and his wife had weekly social engagements with friends, were active in their church, and managed to be wonderful grandparents and great-grandparents. In their 70s, they would pick up the "older people" to take them to church. Those "older people" were other parishioners in their 90s. That always brought a smile to my face. They adopted more of a leisure retirement model and have been able to fund it for more than 35 years. It turned out they had a significant amount of runway left.

I have another friend in central Florida who retired from his corporate job when he was 68, but went into teaching business classes at the local college. He reengaged in the workforce in a different way. He worked fewer hours, but had a significant impact on the students he taught. He brought real world business experience into the classroom and that was a unique quality in his teaching. Although he and his wife had a daughter and son early in their marriage, they had a third child, a daughter, later in life. Raising her when the others were already out of the house sometimes seemed like they were raising an only child. They are also now grandparents to her three young children – a grandson and a set of twin granddaughters. Without their help with the children, their daughter would lose a significant part of her support system. They are now in their 80s and still very active. Again, they have had lots of runway left.

Those who have already walked this path of reinventing themselves later in life are full of wisdom if we choose to listen. I remember going on a trip to Alaska in 2004 with my husband and another couple. We did a land and sea excursion, with the first half of the trip on a cruise ship and the second half on land. It was a beautiful trip, filled with the abundance of nature, the enjoyment of friends, and the delight of getting away from it all. We didn't realize that the travel agency we used to book the trip catered to seniors. We were all around 45 at the time and our fellow guests were delightful to us and fun to be around, but all at least 20 to 30 years older than us. We were on a tour bus toward the end of the trip when an older gentleman sitting with his wife grabbed my arm and said to me, "Do these kinds of things while you are young enough to enjoy them. You never know what will get in your way when you are older." Those words have stuck with me all these years. With each decade, you grow in your wisdom – what you do with that wisdom is your choice.

My point in highlighting these stories is to illustrate just how interesting and lengthy these next chapters of your life can be. You don't know exactly what life holds for you and how it will play out. Some of you will get sandwiched in between your kids and aging parents and experience challenges just keeping up. Wouldn't it be great to choose to do something for yourself and pursue it now, while you can?

These stories also illustrate just how long that "runway" can be. When you began your career, did you contemplate you would be doing the same thing for 30 or even 50 years? I doubt it. Life is made to be lived in cycles, but it's not made to be boring and unfulfilling.

Why Change is So Hard

"People don't resist change; they resist being changed."
Peter Scholtes

Why is it so hard to make meaningful change in your life on your own? The answer is simple. As you got more and more successful, the stakes got higher and higher. You began to feel that a misstep was to be avoided at all cost. Articulating what you want (if you could even identify it) was risky. Taking your foot off the pedal for a while and slowing down didn't feel like an option. Totally changing your direction seemed like an even riskier option. Choices you contemplate when you have already reached a high level of success can seem extremely risky. Sometimes they are, but you have to determine if the risk is really worth the effort.

So, when is the time to start focusing on yourself? How about *now*? I recently saw an ad for an accelerated degree program for adults at a local college. The person in the ad was discussing how her family and friends were telling her she was too old to pursue a degree. They said, "You will be 50 by the time you get your degree." They probably echoed what she had been telling herself all along. But in this ad, her response was magic. She said, "I'll be 50 anyway, I might as well have that degree!" The action of accepting where you are and dismissing objections that don't really matter can be extremely powerful.

I'm not many years away from traditional retirement age. But I cannot imagine stopping what I am doing by then. It's just not an option for me. I can't imagine not being a coach and serving others, or working and volunteering in some capacity. How about you? Are you enjoying what you're doing enough that you'd want to do it beyond traditional retirement age? Or do you envision a different chapter? If so, now's the time to start making it happen.

Your Life Experience Really Matters

"Be brave. Take risks. Nothing can substitute experience."
Paulo Coelho

The effort you have put into your life thus far has so much value. You have endured what life has thrown in front of you and have emerged a stronger, wiser person with a lot to contribute to this world. Once you begin to take in and appreciate what you have to offer, you will hopefully realize you cannot allow these precious gifts to go to waste. You have so much to offer and you should consider continuing to grace others in your life with these wonderful traits and gifts.

When the stakes are high, your decisions are that much more important. It's important to get it right, but if you don't, it won't be the end of the world. I've designed the process in this book to give you options to choose from and an opportunity to make another choice if your current one isn't working out for you.

If you take action, even if it's not quite right for you, you put your brain into a mode of action and healthful energy which stimulates you in a very positive way. Like with exercise, when you start moving, after a while, you want to move and you miss it if you don't.

I fully believe you can start with a desired outcome, but once you put together a plan and start taking action, the path may present additional opportunities for you. One action leads to something else and before you know it, you can have something phenomenal happening. I recommend staying open to the possibilities. The results may surprise and amaze you. Not only will _you_ benefit by taking action, but if you are connected with others, like your family, why not be "the best you" you can be? When you are happier and have more to give, you will become a role model of living well.

When I started considering a new chapter in my life, I assumed no one would want to hear what I had to offer or that I might not have enough "runway" left to realize my most fulfilling next chapter. Neither of those things proved true for me. The reason I was able to overcome those thoughts was simple – I took _action_! I had to get out of my head and into my heart to bust through the negativity I was creating by doubting myself. I had to keep moving forward.

Others will recognize it when you have your life together and are authentically happy and doing what you are meant to do. Here is a recent example from my experience. I was at a gathering with about 20 people of all ages, both men and women. We were there to enjoy a four-course dinner with wine pairings and discussions with different artists. Between each course of the meal, we heard an artist who described his or her work and process. It was fascinating! Seated next to me was a lovely young woman who was in her early 30s. Across from me were the rest of my 50-something women friends who were having a grand time. We were laughing, exchanging photos, and generally having a ball. Later in the evening, I turned to the young lady next to me and asked what she wanted from her life. She quickly said, "I want to be like you ladies!" In the past, I would normally assume I had nothing in common with this younger woman, much less anything to discuss. I no longer feel that way, of course, but her response still surprised me. When I returned home that evening, I gave some thought to what she may have seen by interacting with us. I believe she saw confidence, intelligence, fun, and even a command of handheld technology! We really don't always know what impact we'll have on someone who crosses our path.

What is at stake for you if you decide to do nothing? Well, that's something only you can answer. And again, only you can make a judgment about how high the stakes are in your life; no one else can dictate that for you. At the end of the day, stepping into a new chapter is about being willing to take action and looking at how committed you are to getting the results you desire.

My hope for you is that even if you don't take significant action, the ideas in this book will stimulate your thinking and result in you taking more time for yourself. I want to help you put yourself first so you can learn to enjoy that great blessing in your life.

Chapter 3 – Stepping into Your Purpose Can Get Messy

"Finding and stepping into your purpose can feel like you are shedding everything familiar."
Tina Meilleur

Let Me Prepare You for What's Ahead

I promised I would guide you through this process and be here for you, to prepare you for what's ahead. When you start to explore and engage your imagination, it can be exciting and fun. Let's find out what's possible for you. But how do you know what is in your heart that you've been afraid to acknowledge? I can help you get to that place where acknowledgment of your true desire is possible. That is where beautiful alignment happens. When you step into your purpose, you will feel more energetic, alive, and available for those around you.

I also want you to be prepared for the other emotions that may not feel as good, but may also surface as you begin to explore and take action. As you have become successful, you developed a routine, a way of navigating your life that works for you. That may have become an ingrained habit that is difficult to break, even when breaking it is what you need to do to live more fully.

When you begin to disrupt habitual patterns, your brain sends up warning signals and makes you uncomfortable. Imagine your normal commute to work – you probably expect to take a certain route and arrive at your office within an acceptable range of time. Now imagine you decide to take a scenic route so you can witness the beautiful sunrise. You are so excited to experience this unexpected beauty, but it is quickly extinguished by your anxiety when you realize this route will make you terribly late arriving at your office. Was the beauty worth it? Would viewing the sunrise on this route every morning result in a happier outlook for your entire day? Would it be worth the adjustment in your schedule so you could arrive within that acceptable range of time?

This type of assessment is an example of the heart-based balance I am talking about when it comes to making change and reevaluating habits. The things you select as actions when you decide to move in a different direction aren't necessarily going to be on the path of least resistance for you. That may temper your excitement with a bit of uncertainty and discomfort. And that's okay.

That's why I called this chapter "Stepping into Your Purpose Can Get Messy" – because there's a risk of experiencing some negative emotions. However, knowing that may be a possibility, you can prepare for it. It doesn't take the risk away, but if the associated (and temporary) uncomfortable feelings don't come as a surprise as you push against ingrained habits, you are better equipped to withstand them. Remember that the discomfort is temporary. I promise there is light at the other end of the tunnel.

Let's take a look at how this "messiness" can present itself. It can take many forms. For some people, it can take the form of self-doubt, lack of confidence, or second-guessing decisions. For others, it can take the form of sadness, loss of identity, or isolation. There can be any combination of these or other emotions. The bottom line is that there is no formula. Time and patience are two of your best tools. When you start to make changes to integral parts of your life, like your career or a relationship, you disrupt your foundation as you know it.

There is also another dynamic that occurs. We tend to fear change happening "to" us. You might worry about the loss of a job, or someone ending a relationship with you. When these things happen, they can be really painful. However, when you *choose* to make major changes, you *voluntarily* bring the discomfort into your life. Even if you ask yourself, "Why did I do this to myself?" you know you chose it. There's strength in that.

Your Emotions Will Come in Waves

Be prepared for the ebb and flow of your emotions. You may be tempted to quit, but just know that whatever uncomfortable emotions you're feeling as you go through the process of stepping into your next chapter, they're temporary. Knowing this can help you challenge your thoughts and emotions with your own evidence. This evidence is found in your life experience, in the fact that you have successfully navigated change in the past, and in the promise of achieving what you are working toward.

When you start to step out and begin to make significant changes in your life, it can throw you into a chaotic state. You will begin to question why you want something different, whether it is worth it, and any number of reasons why what you are going after probably won't work out.

Also, when you begin to take steps to make meaningful change, you often leave behind what is comfortable. Your logical brain is used to comfort and will attempt to return to that state, even if what you are attempting will eventually be better for you. Depending on the magnitude of the change, your "survival fear" may kick in. Although it sounds quite negative, it really is a kind way for your brain to protect you from what it may interpret as danger. What your logical brain doesn't know yet, because it hasn't experienced it, is the contentment and sense of achievement you will feel once you have accomplished what you set out to change.

When you experience discomfort or even mild anxiety over what you are about to undertake, you can also make those around you anxious as well. Being aware of this can ease the dynamics with the people in your life as you continue to grow and move closer to what you want.

There's a ripple effect that happens from taking steps to make meaningful change in your life. I could go on and on about how rewarding those changes can be once you execute your plan and are living the way you would like to. Being aware of what can come up for you once you start dreaming and planning, means you won't be taken for a loop.

What Stories Do You Tell Yourself?

When fear inserts itself into your process of dreaming about what you want for yourself, it can call up the history of every negative story you have ever told yourself. These stories can stop you dead in your tracks and convince you of certain failure.

These stories can be powerful in derailing your plans, but I believe if you begin to recognize that (a) the stories will come up and (b) they are only stories and not the truth, you will be on your way to facing this issue head on.

What are some of the stories you tell yourself? Here are some of the common ones I've seen in working with my clients:

- I'll never find love.
- I can't afford to quit my job.
- I'll never get that promotion.
- I'm too old to start my own business.
- I don't know who would hire me.
- I don't know who I can trust.
- I don't have anything to offer.

Maybe you believe there's a prerequisite that must be satisfied before you can take action. This creates a roadblock that gets in your way and prevents you from taking action. It happens when you rationalize that there are certain conditions that must be met in order for you to be able to move forward. Some of the prerequisites I've heard from my clients are:

- I'll be happy when....
- I can't possibly do that until....

- My husband (or wife) would never approve of....
- I can't trust other people because....
- I'm not qualified to do that since I....

The interesting thing about conditions you place in the way of your progress is that unless you see that roadblock for what it is, once the most important one gets satisfied, you will likely find another to put in its place. Take this example: You want to take the steps to realize your dream of becoming an entrepreneur, but you feel your husband or wife would never approve of you starting your own business. You break through your fear and decide to talk to him or her about what you truly want. To your surprise, he/she is very supportive and encourages you to take action. You get so excited and begin to get a glimpse of your new life as an entrepreneur. Your excitement quickly wanes as you begin to worry about another concern. You begin to tell yourself you aren't qualified to start your own business because you haven't done it before. You wonder what qualifications you have or who would hire you. You decide you can't begin until you figure out how to become more qualified.

I'm here to tell you these fears are perfectly *normal*! Many people feel these emotions. You may not know it, particularly if they don't share their feelings very readily, but it's a reality for so many people. If you're able to recognize what is happening as you move toward your dream, it will help you avoid this trap of interminable roadblocks.

Stories you tell yourself can distort your reality and really get in the way of your ability to make the changes required to realize your dreams. The excitement you feel when you are planning to get what you truly want in your life can be quickly replaced with paralyzing fear. Just a glimpse of what is possible in your future may be enough to trigger a strong fear response.

You can also be a victim of your obligations, and these situations can keep you down. Limiting situations may include things like completing an important project at your company, the amount of debt you have, your spouse's career, the ages of your children – the list can go on and on. Don't allow situations to trap you into not taking action. There will always be a "situation" in place that you can use as an excuse. If you recognize the limitation created by the situation at hand, you can work that into your plan and still make things happen.

Are you seeing the pattern? Excitement, fear, excitement, fear. That pattern will be repeated. Knowing how to recognize it allows you to keep going anyway.

How Can You Take Control?

"It is our choices...that show what we truly are, far more than our abilities."
J.K. Rowling

What is at play here is your right to choose. You may feel that your current situation is a result of your choices. If so, why not create a situation you really want by making different choices? When you were younger, your decisions probably didn't carry as much weight as they do now. When you are making decisions for one person, results of those decisions are much easier to endure. When there are more people in your life that may be impacted by what you do, there is much more to consider.

For many of the people I spoke to as I was writing this book, including clients who have undergone these transformations, the majority of them got support from family and friends above and beyond what they expected. Many were nervous to discuss their deep desires and the potential impacts of pursuing and achieving them, but when they did, they were surprised by the reactions of those most important to them. And at the end of the day, the only opinions that count are the opinions of people who love and respect you – and that includes yourself. It doesn't make any difference what mere acquaintances think of what you are doing or the choices you make. Letting go of the need to please everyone can give you a new sense of freedom.

Take control early in the process. Confide in some people who are really close to you and who you think are likely to understand what you want to pursue. Share your desires with them. Don't worry if they don't understand at first. If they care about you, they will want the best for you. I was totally surprised by the support I received from my family and friends when I set out to explore a new next chapter in my life. I won't lie – their support wasn't immediate – but after some time had passed and they saw how committed I was to pursuing my new path, they realized I was serious. At the end of the day, those closest to me saw how happy I was and eventually let go of their doubts. Their hearts were in the right place – they had only wanted to be sure I would be okay.

It's wonderful to have the support of your family and friends, but if they are not involved in what you do or don't fully understand what your new path entails, it is going to be important to find a new tribe. Your new tribe should contain like-minded individuals who share your passion and are either going through what you are going through at the same time or have been there and can mentor you.

I had to learn that I was not alone in my quest. There are so many others who were going through exactly what I was. I mentioned attending an event with 750 other entrepreneurs, mostly women. It was at that event that I began to understand just how many others were out there going through exactly what I was experiencing. It gave me so much comfort knowing that I wasn't alone. I discovered that others in this exclusive tribe were extremely open and giving, and that was unlike anything I had experienced before.

Understand there is a lot of support available if you are open to accepting it.

Pay Attention to the Company You Keep

"Surround yourself with only people who are going to lift you higher."
Oprah Winfrey

I've been associated with a business coach named Suzanne Evans. I followed her for about a year before I started attending some of her events. At one of these events, she was on stage and said, "You are the average of the five people with whom you spend the most time." That one statement caused me to step back and really start to consider with whom I was spending my time and what impact they had on me.

After I completed my review, I decided I wanted to back away from some people with whom I was interacting. I realized they were stuck in their own stories and were trying to pull me into those stories in almost every conversation. I wanted to be supportive, listen to their pain and try to help, but at some point, I realized they didn't really want solutions, nor did they recognize the excuses they had accepted. Those excuses were keeping them in the same spot indefinitely.

As you begin to dream and make plans and then share those thoughts with people around you, be wary of those who contribute reasons why your plans won't work for you. I'm not talking about someone who knows you well enough to know your plan may not be right for you. I'm talking about people who will contribute reasons why you shouldn't pursue your dreams because they have not been successful in realizing their own. Their energy and motives, even if they care about you a great deal, may be too myopic to be of assistance to you.

The best partner for you is someone who can be objective and who doesn't have anything at stake in your situation. Your partner should be able to ask the hard questions and help you drill down into your "why" as well as your commitment to change. Once you have a keen understanding of those, nothing can stop you. If you are having trouble getting support from those around you, you might want to seek out that objective partner as you make this journey.

Many successful people create a springboard to greater success by finding a way to associate with people who are enjoying the success they crave. There are mastermind groups organized around different topics, around solution-seeking, and even around specific business models. These groups are designed to challenge their members under the leadership of someone who has been there and can speak to success strategies.

There are also opportunities for one-on-one coaching, group coaching, and more exclusive mastermind groups. Each one of these options has its own benefits, but only you can make the final decision about what you may need as you go through this process. As a coach, I provide support in each of these areas and help my clients with recommendations about the best fit for them at whatever stage they are in within their own process of designing and achieving their next chapter.

How to Calm Your Inner Critic

"The genius of evolution lies in the dynamic tension between optimism and pessimism continually correcting each other."
Martin E.P. Seligman

When you need to calm your negative thoughts and the destructive self-talk that pops up during your process, start with paying attention. When you can recognize the thoughts and emotions that occur, you can learn how to address and release them. Thoughts and emotions affect each other. Thoughts can trigger emotion, but they can also help us deal with emotion in a rational way. When a negative thought creeps in, there are a couple of quick ways you can become more objective:

Become the "watcher" of the thought.

Back away from the emotion that has become wrapped up in the thought. Ask yourself whether the thought is based in fact or is based in fear or worry. This "watcher" concept puts you on the outside looking in and invites you to detach from the negative outcome with which your emotions are associated.

As an example, if you get extremely worried about opening your own business because you think you won't be successful, I invite you to challenge that thought. If you step back, you can ask yourself whether you have any evidence that you *won't* be successful. If you have never been in business, you simply won't have any evidence and your worry is probably misplaced. You can take the energy you were spending on worry and redirect it to creating a business model that will be as successful as possible.

Realize that you can adjust your emotions associated with the troublesome thought.

When you rationally challenge the thought and find it to be untrue or highly improbable, your emotions can be trained to follow that rationalization of the thought.

If you take the example above, when you begin to challenge whether you have evidence that your own business won't be successful, you find that no evidence exists. Trying to satisfy your need for some proof that your thoughts and emotions are on point, you highlight the statistics of business failures among other new entrepreneurs.

If you can step back as the "watcher," you can then apply the rational concept that no other entrepreneur can run a business the way you will. They may have the same product or service, but each of us is unique in life and certainly in business. No one can predict whether you will succeed or fail with any certainty. To deprive yourself of your dream of owning and running your own successful business would be a travesty, particularly if you make that decision without any evidence to support your position. Instead, gather evidence that you *can* succeed.

* * *

Your next life chapter can be one of your most important, so it will be important to take the time to process the thoughts and emotions that come up as you begin to explore and make plans. Feeling discomfort or doubting the choices you are about to make are two of the key reasons why you may abandon your plans or delay your dreams. In Chapter 4, I'll give you tools to help you overcome obstacles. Being forewarned about what you may experience can increase your chances of success. Your focus and energy will be rewarded by achieving more than you thought was possible at this point in your life.

Chapter 4 – Exploring and Designing Your Next Chapter

"Find what you were meant to do and the rest will unfold in front of you."
Tina Meilleur

When I began to think about helping others go through the process of reinventing their lives or reengaging in a more meaningful way, I realized that I was experienced to assist others in one of their most important life quests because I had reinvented myself again and again, and had become more successful each time.

As I reflected on *how* I did it, I realized there was a process I followed each time I went through a personal life reinvention. I also realized I'd been using this process with my clients, time and time again, although I had not formalized it. Once I understood this process and its effectiveness, articulating it with my coaching clients resulted in even greater successes for them. I formalized the process to make it more easily repeatable and adaptable for each client. Not everyone had the same issues in each step, so being able to customize the process allowed me to offer more support specifically where clients needed it.

That was the breakthrough I needed. At that point, everything started coming together and clients began to have more significant breakthroughs. They were able to get further than ever before in achieving what they truly wanted. Clients who reported quitting or shutting down in the past, before they had truly made the leap to living their true desire for their life, began to use this process to break through the obstacles that had previously stopped them prematurely. And some of them went on to use the process for bigger and bigger achievements.

I'd like to give you an overview of the process, which we'll explore in more detail in subsequent chapters.

Introduction to the CRAVE™ Process

"Craving, not having, is the mother of a reckless giving of oneself."
Eric Hoffer

The process I have designed is called CRAVE. The word "crave" has different meanings, depending on who you ask. The baseline definition I use is from *The Merriam-Webster Dictionary*:

- to ask for earnestly: beg, demand (*crave* a pardon for neglect)
- to want greatly: need (*craves* drugs)
- to yearn for (*crave* a vanished youth)
- to have a strong or inward desire (*craves* after affection)

Use this process as a gift to yourself to help you navigate the process of getting what you have been craving. Approach it with love and the intention to help yourself explore and achieve what you truly want.

In the CRAVE™ process, the letters stand for:

- C – Choose
- R – Reimagine
- A – Act

- V – Validate
- E – Enjoy

I followed these steps, except that I added the "enjoy" step because it's important but it's something I rarely used to include. Once I accomplished something, I was usually on to the next thing without another thought! I've learned, however, that making space for enjoying the things I accomplish makes them that much sweeter.

I eventually chose to put myself first and do something important for myself. I imagined what my life would be like after I had achieved what I wanted to do, and then I took action. Those actions were often only small steps toward my bigger goal. When an action didn't seem right for me, like planning to pursue another degree after my layoff, I took the time to validate whether it was right for me. When it wasn't, I made a different choice and began the CRAVE™ process again.

You may doubt that this process will work for you or think it's too simple to be effective, but give it a chance. I recommend that you attempt to suspend your disbelief as you begin to go through the CRAVE™ process. If you give this process a chance, you will be giving yourself a chance to get what you truly desire as well.

I'll go into each step of the CRAVE™ process in its own chapter, but here's an overview so you can get familiar with the direction you will be taking.

C is for Choose

You will choose to put yourself first, and then create some options to choose from that contain something very important you will pursue for your next life chapter. In this step, you will:

- Dig deep into what you have been craving for yourself
- Get clear about what might be the most gratifying option for you to pursue

R is for Reimagine

Reimagine what your life could be like if you go after what you truly want and it becomes a reality. This is a tremendously fun step that can get very exciting. When you explore what is possible, it really gets your creative juices flowing. It is important in this step to:

- Not hold back – imagine that anything is possible for you
- Stay in the moment and go with your imagination so you don't let negative thoughts creep in – just have fun with it!

A is for Act

You are going to create a plan for going after what you truly want, and take action. It will be important to:

- Align your action commitment with how badly you want to achieve what you have chosen and reimagined for your life
- Remember the helpful tools you will have learned for this step and deploy them when emotions surface that might derail your efforts

V is for Validation

This is the most important step in the process, because it's when you validate how you feel about what you have chosen and the action you are taking. Is it feeling like what you envisioned in the Reimagine step? When doing this step, you will be equipped to determine:

- Whether what you're feeling is simply fear associated with doing something new
- Whether, once you've started taking action, your choice truly seems right for you

E is for Enjoy

Enjoy your wins, or simply celebrate taking action on something that you selected for yourself. For this step, you will:

- Make a list of little rewards for yourself and decide when in your change process you will enjoy your wins with a reward
- Pick something major as a reward for getting through the whole CRAVE™

process and making your next chapter happen.

* * *

The CRAVE™ process is exactly how I made my own life transformations, especially the last one I went through – going from my corporate career to my career as a life and business coach. The process has been proven to work, time and time again. You can use it to create success as you follow your heart toward your own desired transformation.

Is This a Total Do-Over?

"You don't get to choose how you're going to die. Or when. You can only decide how you're going to live. Now."
Joan Baez

What stops you from going after what you truly want? I spoke in the last chapter about the feelings that may come up when you start to make significant change in your life. By going through the CRAVE™ process, you will learn about tools and practices that will help you understand how to respond effectively to your feelings and bust through fear and negativity.

Commit to putting yourself first and taking the time to go through the CRAVE™ process. It may take a bit of time and attention to wrap your head around the negative feelings that may arise, but as you commit you will gain the space and energy to undertake this exploration and step into your best life chapter ever.

Many of my clients had an initial fear that making the changes they wanted to make would turn their life upside down, and they didn't want that to happen. Your focus on change and transformation can be as small or large as you want it to be – and the CRAVE™ process works either way. For me, the layoff from my corporate job was a catalyst, so I had a unique opportunity to decide to do something totally different. For you, the catalyst may be a desire to put more emphasis on fitness and health, or to take more time off, or to take some art classes – whatever your dream is for your next chapter – and whether it feels big or small – the CRAVE™ process will bring you success if you commit to it.

If you want to make a total life transformation, this process will carry you through. Your plan may be more robust due to the magnitude of what you wish to undertake, but the process is equally as exciting and effective, if you lean into it.

Think about a time when you planned a spectacular vacation. You decided which locations were on your list of desired destinations and you began to imagine yourself arriving there and enjoying your luxurious trip and getting away. You went about creating a plan for your trip – and you dreamed about it and imagined it all along the way. You set a date and began your countdown to pure enjoyment. Maybe, at some point, you questioned whether you'd selected the right location. But you eventually moved through that doubt and the departure date of your trip arrived. You went on your trip and realized your dream, which was the outcome of your careful, diligent planning. You luxuriated on your much-needed vacation. You celebrated the results of your efforts and the fabulous environment. The memories you made remain powerful and provide joy to you even today.

Imagine doing that for yourself in your everyday life. Imagine your future as if you had planned a dream vacation, one you will live each day as your new truth, your deepest desire.

Doesn't that sound fabulous? That is the power of focusing on and allowing yourself to get what you truly want. What if you could get you to the point where your life is everything you dreamed of? Wouldn't that make you happy and delighted you made the commitment to yourself?

You won't need to be alone in your quest. You can find others who share the vision of going after what they truly want from their life, and doing so will increase your chances of success. What if you had a tribe of like-minded people who were also reimagining their life and going through the process of stepping into their next chapter? You can join the tribe of the Your Next Chapter Book Group, where we gather to support each other in a safe place. You can ask questions and get answers or just share how you are feeling as you go through the process. I encourage you to join the community on Facebook. Search for "Your Next Chapter Book Group".

The CRAVE™ Process –

A Case in Point

What better way to help you feel comfortable with this process than to illustrate how it has worked for others? Even before I had a name for the steps of this process, I saw it in action in other people's lives.

Here is a case in point. Deb worked for a large manufacturing company at the beginning of her career. She worked with predominantly male counterparts in engineering and was a star at analysis, presentations, and strategy development. Of course, being a star in those areas meant she knew how to frame difficult subjects, facilitate solutions, and properly communicate them. Deb watched as her male counterparts took expensive extended vacations while she was left to perform all of the work that, in her view, helped create her co-workers' personal wealth as they continued to get promoted and expanded their earnings. She contributed greatly to their professional and financial success.

The company felt the need to communicate with the public and other stakeholders more directly about their operations, so they created an internal speakers' bureau. Deb participated in the bureau from its inception and received training in delivering the company's message effectively. Her participation was in addition to her regular role, so her plate was quite full. She began traveling to speak on behalf of the company and realized she loved it. When she was in front of an audience, she felt alive and living in her brilliance. She had a real gift for engaging and connecting with the audience.

During her career at this company, Deb pursued a Master's Degree in Business Administration. She now had additional credentials, making her even more valuable than before.

As she watched her counterparts become more and more successful, even beyond the success she had achieved, she had the realization "that could be me." So she chose to put herself first and chose to focus on creating her own business (the Choose step of the CRAVE™ process). She reimagined her life as a business owner, one who would be in charge of her own fate (the Reimagine step). She created a longer-term exit plan along with the action steps she would need to take to realize her dream (the Act step).

She shared her plans with no one except her husband and one other professional confidante. She put together financial spreadsheets and worked to pay down her debt, all while setting aside operating capital with which to start her own business.

Deb joined several professional organizations and made valuable contacts along the way, all while continuing to fulfill her duties at the company. It was as if she was living a double life – she went to the office or traveled for the speakers' bureau during the week and worked to fulfill her future dreams on the weekends. Double-agent Deb continued at the office as if nothing else was going on for her.

Her timetable for making the leap was adjusted several times, but she remained resolute. She went over her plans carefully with her husband so they could agree about when the time was right. She finally decided it was her time and she pulled the trigger on forming her company, leaving the company, and "going live" with her dream. She followed the plan she had created many years ago. Although there were several adjustments to the timeline and the format of her business (the Validate step), she remained committed to taking action. She has now had her own company for 20 years.

She told me her story so brilliantly and with so much enthusiasm, but she was also quick to tell me that during those 20 years there were some months when there were more days than dollars. Even so, she has no regrets. She also is a great example of enjoying success (the Enjoy step). She has the flexibility to stay involved in her community and spend time with her husband and family.

She's a great example of the CRAVE™ process in action. She was not a client and she undertook her plan well before I even envisioned the CRAVE™ steps and decided what to call them. But when I heard her story, I recognized how similar her process was to what I have followed and saw how these steps could work for others.

The keys to Deb's success were many. She had an unflinching commitment to create her own successful business and fulfill her dream. She confided in only those who would understand her dream and support her in achieving it. She also tapped into her unique magnetism and too many skills to list here. She committed to learning what she needed to learn in order to secure business from sectors that were difficult to penetrate. She doesn't do all the work herself, but has created a network of professionals on whom she can rely for quality performances. Those people – her trusted resources – know how she works and they respect her professional standards.

Deb has become a friend and I feel her pride when she tells her story. There's a gleam in her eye as she recounts putting herself first, formulating her dream, creating a plan to make it happen, and continually adjusting her business to make it the right fit for her.

Deb is a wonderful example of making a commitment to a dream and not allowing thoughts and emotions to get in the way. Did she have doubts? Of course. Did she ever think of quitting? Sure. But she forged ahead and didn't allow self-doubt or fear to stand in her way. She also recognized the value of her skills and experience and believed that others needed what she had to offer.

Another wonderful thing about Deb is that she is invested in the success of others. She pays her success forward every day. She has taken other professionals under her wing and helped them realize their own dreams. She believes we all rise together. And we do.

* * *

We all know how to do this – how to go after and get what we want. Sometimes we get comfortable and complacent and forget how we became successful. The CRAVE™ process brings you back to a process that you instinctively already know. As you go through the steps you will also get to revisit the times and the ways you went after what you wanted earlier in your life – and succeeded. That will give you the evidence you need to convince yourself you can accomplish what your heart desires. Starting now.

The next chapters of the book are dedicated to deeper coverage of each step of the CRAVE™ process. If you want to join the Facebook group, search for "Your Next Chapter Book Group".

Your Next Chapter is where things really begin to get fun, so let's get started!

Chapter 5 – You Get to Choose!

"Own your choices, but recognize none of them is permanent."
Tina Meilleur

The "C" in the CRAVE™ process stands for "Choose." This is the first step in the process of designing your next chapter and getting what you want in your future. This is an exploratory step and one that can be very exciting for you if you remain open to what this exploration can do for you.

Since you are interested in exploring your next life chapter, I can assume you are ready to make some important choices. Let's start with the first one – choosing to put yourself first. Is that a difficult one for you? If so, I'm here to help you believe you have no other choice than to make yourself a priority!

Let's begin to examine how you got to where you are. At some point, did you start making choices that put you as a low priority? Did doing that get easier over time, where your needs and wants no longer mattered as much? Over time, did this contribute to feelings of unhappiness, overwhelm, and despair? Did you rationalize and tell yourself things such as, "I'll be able to do that when...."? Did you put qualifiers on the things you want for yourself? But then, when the qualifier you'd placed on your dream – the reason you told yourself to wait – finally went away, you didn't have any problem putting another in its place, right?

As you start this process, please commit to putting yourself first. Let's agree that this is extremely necessary to your success in shaping a new future for yourself. Try it out – it will be liberating!

Why Are Choices So Important?

Making a choice is the first important step toward achieving the life of your dreams. Without the clarity of choice, you won't have clarity of direction. As you get older, you have more choices and options. I used to say, "The good news is that I have a lot of options, the bad news is that I have a lot of options." The interesting thing about making choices is that you already possess that skill - you know how to make them – you've been making them all your life. You chose what college to attend, what job to take, and if you chose to get married, you also chose your spouse. And then there is the choice to have children or not. None of these choices are insignificant, are they?

You may have wrestled with making some of these choices, but in the end, you did make a choice and lived with it. Most of these life choices may have seemed easy for you, but the implications extended into your life today. So, use your journal or The Your Next Chapter Companion Guide you downloaded to answer these questions:

- What is a big decision you remember that you made that worked out well?
- What elements of your decision-making process contributed to that success?
- What is a big decision you made that didn't work out?
- What do you think was responsible for this decision not working out for you?
- How did you recover from that decision?

You've probably made choices you regret, but frankly, once a decision is made, it's done. Once it's done, and it doesn't work out, you either make some adjustments or you have to move on. You can't change the past. You may spend a lot more time ruminating about the choices that didn't work out instead of the ones that worked out well. It may be your nature to focus on the things you might have done better.

- What have you learned from the major life decisions you have made in the past?
- How can you apply those learnings to your future decision-making process?
- How will you stop focusing on those decisions that didn't work out? And how else could you have used that energy?

Your New Paradigm for Decision-Making

Perhaps the older you get, the more you seek safety. Making decisions that pose little risk may become your norm. You may be making decisions quickly based on the speed of your life. If so, you aren't giving them much thought, you are simply making them quickly and moving on.

We are going to dig a bit deeper within this step of the CRAVE™ process. You will be focused on conscious decision-making. It is best if you are fully aware during this process and in touch with what is most important to you.

What Are Your Core Personal Values?

Start in this important place of identifying your own core values. This is a place that will help inform your ultimate decision and determine if it is working for you. It is a place of deep understanding of the real you and what makes you tick. So, let's get started on how you will identify the life choice you wish to pursue.

The first question to ask yourself will help identify and capture your real essence in life. So take some time to think about and answer the following question as honestly as possible: *What are your personal core values?*

Use your journal or the Your Next Chapter Companion Guide and list your values. Take time to dig deep and really get in touch with what you absolutely need to have in place as values in order to make changes in your life. Stay personal with this exercise. Don't get clouded with what is important to those around you; stay with what is most important for you.

You may be able to clarify your personal values quickly, or you may struggle a bit. If you are struggling, here are some questions to stimulate your thinking process:

- What is most important to you personally as you have lived your life?
- In the past, when have you felt the most alive? What values were at play in those situations?
- What traits do others admire in you? Feedback is often a window into aspects of ourselves we rarely think about. Ask those important to you – and then accept and respect the answers.

Your list of core values can be as short or as long as you wish. You can use words like integrity, honesty, giving, adventure, respect, personal growth, freedom, creativity, etc. However, your list should include only those values that really resonate with *you*. Don't give into the temptation to list what you think others would like to read. This is *your* list – make it personal!

After I was laid off and began my own planning process, I did this exercise as I contemplated the choices available for my new career. I recognized that my corporate career had become misaligned with my personal values. Before doing this exercise, I didn't realize the impact that had on my efforts to "show up" every day. After the layoff, I had the opportunity to design something new. My list of values included integrity, risk-taking, freedom, serving others, flexibility regarding both schedule and location, and wealth. These values have formed the basis of every decision I have made since I identified them.

What Do You Dream About?

In your most quiet moments, what do you dream about? This is where you can begin to dig even a little deeper. Your quiet time should be the time you can get in touch with your innermost thoughts – the ones you push down each day as you go about getting things done for everyone else. If you are reading this and chuckling because you don't have any quiet time, well, maybe you have just identified your first choice.

Identify what you dream about in your most quiet moments. You can complete these phrases if they help you:

- If I had the time, I would....
- If I could do anything I want, I would.....
- If I didn't have responsibility for anyone else, I would....
- If I didn't have to worry about hurting anyone's feelings, I would....

You may be the type of person who has more concerns about what you _won't_ get done in your life. If so, identify what you dread in your most quiet moments. You can complete these phrases if they help you:

- If I hadn't _____, I would have lived my life unfulfilled.
- If I never accomplish _____, I will not have achieved what I want in my life.
- If I never get to _____, I'm not sure what my legacy will be.

Finding Your Most Pressing Problem

"A problem well put is half solved."
John Dewey

Now that you have articulated your core values and have uncovered the things you either dream about or dread not getting done in your quietest moments, you are ready to find your most pressing problem. This is about making a choice that you would like to pursue for yourself.

Now that you have this information, what is the most pressing problem you would like to solve for yourself? If you can begin with a specific problem, it is easier to find a solution.

Imagine going into your doctor's office and she asks, "What's wrong?" You reply, "I don't know; everything hurts." She would be hard-pressed to formulate a diagnosis on such a broad complaint. Get very specific about what you would like to change so you can continue to work through the process and plan to make that happen.

What from your "dream" or "dread" lists would you most like to accomplish in your next life chapter? It can be small or large, practical or lofty – the CRAVE™ process works for any size of dream. If you can't decide, take the list of items from your "dream" and/or "dread" lists and rank them according to how you feel when you think about each of them and how important each one feels to you and your future happiness.

These were my top items from my "dream" and "dread" lists:

- **Dream list:** "If I could do anything I wanted, I would have my own business with the flexibility to work anywhere and help as many people as possible by helping them with what I have learned in my life and career – how to navigate the challenges in their lives and businesses. I would help them redefine success on their terms, reinvent themselves, and make their next chapter in life the best one so far."
- **Dread List:** "If I never get to experience the freedom to use my gifts and talents to help others succeed rather than helping only the companies I've worked for succeed, I would not feel I had lived my life's true purpose."

When I said my top item from my dream list out loud, I got a big smile on my face. I also pictured others who were now living the life they were meant to live and were happier because of it. When I thought about my top dread, I had very different feelings. I felt gratitude and pride when I thought of helping people rather than being part of a company with a product.

With your most important items identified, you can move on to stating your most pressing problem. Based on your top-ranked items, take a few minutes and state your most pressing problem: "I would like to make the changes necessary in my life to solve my most pressing problem, which is _____." You will use this as the basis for the rest of the process and in your action plan.

Here is how I stated my most pressing problem as I started the CRAVE™ process: "I would like to make the changes necessary in my life to solve my most pressing problem. I'm too young to retire, so I feel I need to go back into another high-powered corporate role, but I have strong feelings pulling me to work for myself and try to make a difference in other people's lives. How can I create a business that will allow me to serve others and create enough revenue for me to continually serve more people with my message?"

With each step in the CRAVE™ process, I got a bit more specific about my problem statement. I knew I had a lot more productive years to work and it was necessary that the work be in the service of others. I also knew it had to be a business that would fund itself and allow me to have enough revenue to continue to serve more and more people with my message.

How Do You Get Specific?

Let's review what you've done so far. You have:

1. Stated your personal core values
2. Identified the items you either "dream of accomplishing" or "dread not accomplishing" in your life
3. Stated your most pressing problem

In order to go through the rest of the process, you will need to get very specific about your potential choices. You can list more than one, but you will then pick one as your priority. The one you pick must be specific and you must be committed to taking action to achieve it.

Begin by filling in this Next Life Chapter Declaration: "In my next life chapter, I will be _____, so I can_____. When I am successful in _____, I will feel_____.
Whenever I feel stuck while going after this dream, I will remember this feeling of _____, and use it to propel me forward in achieving my heart's desire."

Here was my own Next Life Chapter Declaration that I wrote before I began my business. This declaration became the basis for my own personal reinvention plan: "In my next life chapter, I will be a life and business coach, so I can help others bring their lives and/or businesses to the next level. When I am successful in helping them design and achieve their next chapter, I will feel honored to be of service and proud in having successfully created my own next life chapter. Whenever I feel stuck while going after this dream, I will remember these feelings of honor and pride and use them to propel me forward to achieving my heart's desire."

Your Next Life Chapter Declaration becomes the new story that you craft for your future. You *choose* what you want and design your future your way. It is a conscious decision and one that you own. You are in control of your future destiny because you took the time to put yourself first and focus on what YOU want.

What Do You Have to Offer?

As you get older, your options may become more robust and perhaps more plentiful, although you may not see your life that way. You may feel you are limited in what you can go after. But what if your options are actually exponential? Through the sheer effort of living your life, you have gained valuable experience. You have developed skills that will elevate you through good and bad times. And best of all, you have a richness of navigating your life through preparation and execution of the choices you have made. Below is a motivating story about Mary Kay Ash that illustrates a woman taking advantage of her gifts and talents and becoming more successful than she ever dreamed.

You may be familiar with Mary Kay Ash, the founder and namesake of Mary Kay Cosmetics. As a 45-year-old, hard-working single mother of three, she had a lot at risk. She had worked her way up to the position of National Training Director for a large direct sales company, but knew she was blocked from going any further up the ladder. She quit her job in protest in the early '60s after a gentleman she had trained received a promotion she should have gotten. She knew she had great experience in building traditional direct sales organizations and she knew how to sell to other women. With those skills and an abundance of self-confidence, she began Mary Kay Cosmetics. Within a year, the company hit one million dollars in sales. She kept her core values at the center of her business and made sure she ran the company with those values in clear focus.

The first important choice she made was to put herself first and commit to taking action. Her second most important choice was to start her own business. Had she stayed and decided to settle, all of us would have missed seeing a fantastic female business role model in action.

One of the most intriguing parts of her business model involved uplifting women and supporting them in their business growth. She was one of the first to invest in women and take the time to really teach them to run a business.

Mary Kay Ash understood, with unwavering certainty, what she had to offer. She knew she could sell and she knew she could teach others to be equally effective in the direct sales arena. She provided a platform on which women could not only learn, but be rewarded for their hard work and business skills.

Here's how she executed some of the steps of the same process you're going through:

- She identified her core values
- She chose to put herself first
- She made a choice to start her own business
- She identified and was confident about what she had to offer

You have so much to share in this world. Can you, like Mary Kay Ash did, accept your gifts and talents and make sure you are using them to the fullest extent you can? I believe you can, because I believe these things about you:

- You are important enough to be a priority
- You are talented enough to do anything you want to do
- You deserve to be happy
- You can accomplish anything you set your mind to do

* * *

Take some time to reflect on your work in this chapter. If you honestly answered the questions, they should be providing a lot of insight into your true desires and mindset, as well as valuable evidence about how you have handled decisions and their outcomes in the past.

Learn from the past, but don't allow yourself to think you that you cannot think and act differently in designing your next chapter. Be brave in your choices and resolute in your commitment!

Let's move on now to the next step – R is for Reimagine.

Chapter 6 – Let Your Imagination Guide You

"Your imagination is like a gift; you must open it to be able to enjoy it."
Tina Meilleur

The second step of the CRAVE™ Process is "R" for "Reimagine." This step is so much fun. I will ask you to really engage in this part of the process with childlike wonder. Remember when you were young and you were asked what you wanted to be when you grew up? Didn't you always have a quick answer? When I was really young, my answer was always, "I want to be a ballerina." I had pictures of ballerinas neatly framed and hanging on my bedroom wall. They were the first things I saw when I opened my eyes and the last things I saw before the lights went out. I would dance around in all my clumsiness, not aware of how to properly execute any of the ballet steps, but when I was in my little girl dream, it made me happy.

That's the feeling I want you to capture in this chapter. Call up your dreams without concern or doubts about whether you will get it perfect. I will give you some exercises to help your imagination come through, but first, I'd like you to know why this step is so critical.

I would venture to guess you have pushed your own dreams down for a long time, all in the spirit of helping others fulfill theirs. In order to create your next life chapter in a way that feels authentic for you, you will need to understand and feel how satisfying your life can be if you begin to pursue the choice you made in Chapter 5, during the Choose step. To do this, you will go deep into your imagination, below the surface of your desires. You have already been digging deep, so you should still be in the exploration mode. In Chapter 5, you finally chose to put yourself first, right? So as we begin this step, you are beautifully positioned to let your imagination run wild.

A few ground rules before we get started:

- Suspend all negative thoughts that surface – you can write them down, but don't let them spoil your dream state.
- Don't get lost in whether your choice is right for you yet; based on the work you have already done, it should be a representation of your heart's desire.
- There will be lots of opportunities to adjust later in the process, so don't get bogged down in "getting it perfect" before you begin.
- If you get stuck, you can use some tools I'll share later to help you remove those blocks. Or you can reach out in the Facebook group if you need more help. Search for "Your Next Chapter Book Group".

"The best and most beautiful things in the world cannot be seen or even touched. They must be felt with the heart."

Helen Keller

Begin by getting deeper into your imagination, really digging deep to see what's in your heart, so you get a glimpse into how you will feel once you achieve your new life chapter. You can use your journal to record your thoughts as you move through this step.

We'll begin with your completed Next Life Chapter Declaration from Chapter 5, which is this, but with the blanks filled in to make it personal to you:

"In my next life chapter, I will be _____, so I can_____.
When I am successful in _____, I will feel_____.
Whenever I feel stuck while going after this dream, I will remember this feeling of _____, and use it to propel me forward in achieving my heart's desire."

Close your eyes and imagine how your life would be if you were living what you described in your Next Life Chapter Declaration. Imagine and feel some details about a typical day in your next life chapter:

Doesn't this sound wonderful to explore right now? Inviting a desired future state is a great way to spend your valuable time for a little while. Think about how you will be interacting with those around you in your new chapter. You may have touched on some of this when you went through your typical day exercise, but go a little deeper now. You can use these prompts, if they help you:

- How much more available are you, both physically and emotionally, for those you love? Describe this in enough detail so you can get a feel for the impact of your change.
- How do you feel physically? Do a scan of your body from head to toe and write down how you feel in some detail.
- Do you have more energy? Describe how your energy has shifted and how you might feel more relaxed and/or positive.
- Are you able to manage your negative emotions in a more reasonable way? Describe how you have been able to recognize the negative emotions and deal with the discomfort they create.
- Do those around you seem happier to be around you? Describe the differences you are noticing in your interactions with them.

You can use any other questions or prompts that might give you the information you are seeking, and jot down some notes. You will be able to use these notes later in the process.

Here's how I responded to this step, beginning with my own Next Life Chapter Declaration and then going into what I imagined a typical day would be like:

"In my next life chapter, I am a life and business coach, so I can help others bring their lives and/or businesses to the next level. When I am successful in helping them design and achieve their next chapter, I feel honored to be of service and proud in having successfully created my own next life chapter. Whenever I felt stuck while going after this dream, I remembered these feelings of honor and pride and used them to propel me forward to achieving my heart's desire.

A typical day now is very different from one in my previous world. I wake up early to either exercise or have a morning ritual, like writing or reading. I then work in my home office assisting clients with their dreams and helping them reframe the things that get in the way of their progress. Since I work from home, I have time for regular dinners with my family, where we all sit down at once and discuss the day. I relax in the evening with my husband or conduct evening appointments with clients. When I reflect on my day, I feel gratified and humbled by being of service to others. I sleep soundly because I'm doing what I'm meant to do, and I wake up every day energized and grateful to be doing what I love."

Now it's your turn. Review your Next Life Chapter Declaration and the notes you jotted about your typical day when you are living what you have declared for your next life chapter. Respond to the prompts below to learn more about yourself and what you imagine.

1. Take a moment to read Your Next Life Chapter Declaration and your description of your typical day out loud.
2. How does it make you feel? Jot down some of these feelings.
3. What is your "why" for taking on this challenge? State this in a short sentence or two.
4. What would you feel if you had gotten through the discomfort to make it happen and you finally

achieved what you declared? Write down what comes up for you.

5. What would have to be in place for you to know you were successful in reaching the next life chapter you declared? Make a quick list (you will use this as a starting point in the action step later in the process).

6. If you were to describe yourself in the context of your new life chapter to a close friend or relative, what would you say? Write that down in a short paragraph.

Remember that sharing your thoughts about your next life chapter can be a powerful motivator, particularly if you share it with others. If you're uncomfortable sharing it broadly, you can share it with a few people who are close to you and believe in what you can accomplish.

You are well on your way now to creating a strong foundation for your Next Life Chapter plan. You are well prepared, so let's move on to Chapter 7 and get started with your action plan for turning your dream into your reality. This is where things get really exciting!

Chapter 7 – Anything Is Possible with Action

"The beauty of taking action is that it creates momentum to propel you forward more quickly."
Tina Meilleur

Wow! You have done a lot of work already to craft your next life chapter. How is it feeling? Pretty exciting? Scary? Both answers are okay. Anything worth having is worth a little discomfort, but I hope the excitement is greater than the discomfort.

This chapter – "A" is for "Act" – is where you will realize how achieving your next life chapter is possible. This is where the rubber meets the road and you will be able to see the path upon which this will become a reality. You will move from simply having a dream you have held in your heart, to a reachable, attainable plan. You will be designing your future. Rather than letting it simply happen *to* you, you will be designing it *for* you. If you have ever had an article of clothing altered to fit or had a garment made specifically for you, that is what we are doing here. We are customizing your future to fit the real you.

In this chapter, you will be gathering notes to incorporate into the plan you will be creating. You will be getting your mindset in a place to accept the concepts of saying "yes" and exploring opportunities that you might not have recognized or pursued in the past. And finally, you will learn to manage your emotions associated with making meaningful change in your life.

The change you are pursuing can be as big or small as you wish – the CRAVE™ process works either way. You don't have to turn your whole life upside down in order to be successful. This process is about gaining some control over the type of change you want and the rate at which you want to change. You may want to make a change that's a 180 degree turn and do something totally different with your life. Or maybe you would love to simply leave your office at a reasonable hour and have more balance in your life.

Whatever is your deepest desire, you won't achieve it without a plan and this is the chapter that will get you through the development of that plan.

The Power of Yes

"Say yes, and you'll figure it out afterwards."
Tina Fey

Shonda Rhimes, the well-known, successful creator, head writer, and executive producer of television series such as *Grey's Anatomy, Private Practice*, and the political thriller series *Scandal,* has written a new book called the *Year of Yes: How to Dance It Out, Stand In the Sun and Be Your Own Person.* I saw her interviewed by Oprah recently. In that interview, she talked about her painful introversion, her terror around having difficult conversations, and how she always declined invitations that others would leap to accept.

She spent a year saying "yes" to almost every invitation she could attend. She forced herself to leave the house and engage in the world. She appeared on *Jimmy Kimmel Live!* and gave a commencement speech at Dartmouth. She learned to say yes to play, yes to her health, and yes to exploring how it would feel to say "yes." She told Oprah how much freedom she felt once she started to say "yes." She also could not believe how many opportunities came her way as a result of her simply "showing up."

That can be the power of "yes" for you. You have already said "yes" to putting yourself first, and "yes" to imagining your future. Now I want you to say "yes" to creating a plan and committing to taking *action*. I also want you to be prepared to say "yes" when there is an opportunity that seems consistent with your plan.

I'm asking you to get in the mindset of remaining open to saying "yes" and willing to receive what comes your way. Be prepared to let go of the roadblocks you are putting in your own way. Practice saying "yes" to the right things and "no" to the things that will distract you from your plan.

The Role of Opportunity

"Opportunities don't often come along. So, when they do, you have to grab them."
Audrey Hepburn

You don't have to be given an opportunity in order to do something great. There are other ways to achieve greatness. You can create your own opportunities, or recognize opportunities when they come around. Are you so focused on your day-to-day activities that you wouldn't recognize an opportunity if it hit you in the face? Let's include being on the lookout for and recognizing opportunities as part of your Next Chapter process. In addition, you will be prepared to create your own opportunities.

According to the definition in the *Merriam-Webster Dictionary*, "opportunity" is defined as "a favorable juncture of circumstances" or "a good chance for advancement or progress." Creating a plan for achieving your Next Life Chapter Declaration puts you on the path to meaningful change by making you more aware of opportunities, so you can take advantage of the right opportunities for you or create "a favorable juncture of circumstances."

When I hear that phrase, "a favorable juncture of circumstances," I immediately think of planets aligning, the universe giving you what you want – all because you're open to receiving what comes your way. When you are open to what is happening around you and are aware enough to recognize when conditions are right for something great, you will be unstoppable.

One of the things that distinguishes super achievers from average achievers is the way they handle opportunities.

"To hell with circumstances; I create opportunities."
Bruce Lee

Your Next Life Chapter plan will include ways to create opportunities, and you will need to include flexibility in your plan so that you can take advantage of the opportunities that present themselves and are a good fit for you. Here are some questions you can ask yourself around creating opportunities:

- When others come to me for help, what is the common theme of their requests?
- What do I do in my life or career that feels like absolute joy and causes me to lose track of time?
- What have I noticed as a significant problem or gap in some particular area, but know that I possess the skill and experience to solve that problem or address that gap?

Your answers can help you identify areas within which you can create opportunities based on your skills and talents. What came up for you? What opportunities do you see for specific focus areas in your new life chapter? Do you need to dedicate some time to these areas of interest and talent so you will be in an even better position to notice and accept opportunities that come along? If anything really struck you in this exercise, make a note of it so you can incorporate it into your plan.

Managing Emotions

One of the risks of putting together a plan is that once you see it in context and realize it can become a reality for you, other emotions start to surface. You can experience joy and celebrate because you can see your future or you step back in fear because your plan seems overwhelming.

One of the ways to control that overwhelm is to focus only on the steps you need to take next. Even small steps can pay big dividends. The beauty of this planning process is to create small steps you can do each day, and then each week, to keep your momentum going.

View your plan as a means to making your dream a reality. Your plan is the structure that gives you the freedom to go after what you want. It becomes the connection between you and your dream. If you take action on the steps in your plan, I guarantee you will move forward toward your dream and achieve the future you desire. Even if your emotions are sometimes overwhelming, you will know you're moving in the right direction. It will help if you can commit to treating the plan you are about to create as a positive foundation that you can lean on throughout this process.

If this process is daunting for you, I understand. In my own planning process, I felt a great deal of overwhelm. I realized it was because I hadn't gotten the steps small enough to control the overwhelm. I had always been a "big picture" person and very strategic. I could often get a lot done without a robust plan simply by doing things based on my experience. But when I became an entrepreneur I had to adapt my skills for a new environment, and I quickly learned that "winging it" was not my best option.

Productive Steps

One of the things I had to come to terms with was not getting immediate results when I executed a step. I should have known better, because in my corporate role, everything I touched took multiple months or years to come to fruition. I worked on very large initiatives, usually transforming groups or processes as a change agent. Implementing change can be very slow – particularly in a large company.

I've learned that every productive step we take is not wasted. Notice I said "productive step." You can find ways to avoid doing what you dread doing, but if you stay focused on steps that can move you closer to your goal, you will get there more quickly, even if it takes a while. You may discover that the opportunities that come your way are worth staying focused on making productive steps.

I am often amazed by how taking a simple step can result in opportunities I had not envisioned. For example, I once gave a speech to about 200 women, and the resulting opportunities surprised me. My message seemed to resonate with them and I had many requests for follow-up based on that speech. Women reached out to me for information about groups I run, other speaking opportunities, and opportunities for collaboration.

When you put yourself first and take the next step toward your goal, you're likely to be surprised by the ripple effect of your action. Those ripples will become waves of change that can help you create your successful next life chapter.

Pulling Your Plan Together

Let's get specific about how you start creating your action plan. Each of the steps below will take you closer to action and the excitement of turning what you have been imagining into a life you are living.

Step 1 – Complete Your Declaration

Begin with your completed Next Life Chapter Declaration from Chapter 5, with the blanks filled in:

"In my next life chapter, I will be _____, so I can_____.
When I am successful in _____, I will feel_____.
Whenever I feel stuck while going after this dream, I will remember this feeling of _____, and use it to propel me forward in achieving my heart's desire."

How does your declaration feel to you? You're comfortable with it, right? If you're not quite yet, share it with a few close friends or family members and practice saying it out loud. That is what worked for me. I had a hard time letting go of my corporate identity and declaring myself a life and business coach, so I practiced saying it out loud to friends and family, then started attending some networking events and saying it to those people. Eventually, I became comfortable with it – mainly because I trained myself to own it. You own your declaration when you get excited about it and can't wait to tell people what makes you who you are.

Step 2 – List the Big Steps

List the big steps you will need to take to achieve what you have chosen in your declaration. These will be your milestones, the points at which you will really celebrate! For each milestone, be sure to set a target completion date. This requires you to estimate how long each milestone will take.

Allow enough time to complete this step, without using the importance of this step as an excuse to drag it out. Include some steps that are not dependent on any of these items you might view as a constraint. This will ensure that you keep moving.

Here are some questions that may help, along with examples of milestones:

- Do you need any additional training in order to achieve what you have chosen? ("Take a photography class" or "Finish my PhD")
- Are there major opportunities you should explore based on your declaration? ("Follow up with my

contact in the alumni/ae office" or "Volunteer in an organization that is close to what I want to do in my next chapter")

- Are there any other major life changes that will need to be made to support your choice? ("Move closer to downtown" or "Get an internship in an accounting firm")
- Do you need major funding to accomplish what you have chosen? ("Create a crowdfunding request" or "Write a formal business plan")
- Are there any other major shifts that must happen for you to move forward? ("Get my family on board with my plan" or "Cut back on the hours I spend at my job")
- Are there any major constraints that must be resolved before you can achieve your goal? ("Finish the house remodel" or "Get my son enrolled in college")

Step 3 – Choose Your Celebrations

For each milestone you listed, choose how you're going to celebrate when you accomplish that milestone. Won't that be fun?

- List all the ways you like to celebrate.
- Match a specific celebration with each milestone.
- Allocate a celebration budget to fund your milestone celebrations.

Step 4 – List the Smaller Steps

For each milestone, what are the smaller steps you need to take to make it happen? For example, if you listed "Take a photography class" as a milestone, your smaller step might be:

- "Call the photography studio I like and ask for class recommendations."
- "Look at class listings online."
- "Register for the class."
- "Attend the first class."

Don't sweat the details of your plan. You can get as detailed as you wish beneath each milestone. The milestones will be your guide for your plan. If you're not a person who thrives on detail, you will be fine with just the milestones.

Step 5 – Finalize Your Plan

Take a break from your plan and let it sit overnight or use your own judgment about your time frame. It should be long enough to allow you to get your head around the steps you have outlined, but not long enough for you to lose momentum! After your break, go back and review it, make changes, and finalize it! This will be a proud moment and one that is worth celebrating!

* * *

Even though Step 5 asks you to finalize your plan, it will always be a work in progress. You will continue to tweak it as new options are revealed. You will learn, as you start taking action, that opportunities may surface that will cause you to change direction.

This is your plan, so keep it updated so it will continue to guide you well. It's designed to get you going and keep you on track.

Train Yourself to Take Action

"The way to get started is to quit talking and begin doing."
Walt Disney

Now that you have a plan, you're all set, right? Maybe not. If you have difficulty with taking action, that's good to be aware of. When you start to get closer to achieving what you really want, fear may set in and you can start to shut down. Focus on completing small steps and celebrating along the way. Don't worry about the big picture – just do the smaller steps you have laid out for yourself, for now. You will soon get more comfortable as you start seeing your cumulative progress – I promise!

You can also train yourself to take action. Taking action is just like any other habit. Repetition is the key for establishing a new habit. Here are some pointers that may help you create a habit of action:

- ***Don't wait for perfection.*** Neither your plan nor the conditions in your

137

life will ever be perfect. Everything you think you need to be in place in order to move ahead probably won't ever be in place. If you begin by simply taking action, perfection will not matter as much. Try it. You will see.

- *Use action to combat fear.* When fear comes up, taking action is a quick way to work through it. More than likely, your fear is a result of a belief about what could happen. Taking action quickly moves you to the reality of what is happening, rendering your fear invalid.

- *A dream is just a dream.* A dream is just a dream until you take action to make it real. The longer a dream stays in your head and heart unfulfilled, the harder it will be to believe it can ever be real.

- *Live for today.* You cannot change the past and, although you are planning for your future, you cannot predict it with accuracy, so live for today. Ask yourself, "What can I do today to move closer to my dream?" Focus on the next step that you can do *today*. Inevitably, tomorrow will turn into next week, and then next month. Unless you take action, your time frame will turn into never!

Now that you have a plan and the tools for busting through when taking action feels scary or challenging, what else might come up? What do you think might keep you from being and staying excited about taking action on your dream?

Fear is the quickest killer of excitement, but what if you could blend those two emotions? I have learned to do that in many situations, especially when I am facing something new that I really want but I'm really scared. When this happens, I say I'm "scare-cited" – I'm scared but excited at the same time. I use that feeling to propel myself forward by reminding myself of what I'm trying to accomplish and staying focused on that. I know that if I can just get through a few more of the steps required on the way to my goal, the scales will tip and I'll become more excited than scared.

Pick something in your plan that is exciting but scary and go through this exercise:

- Pick a step that seems particularly scary for you and important for your progress.
- What about that step scares you the most?
- Since this step is so important to your progress, can you remind yourself of the dream life you are working to create? Take a few moments and articulate how this step can help you get there.
- Can you focus on celebrating your recognition of the fear and remind yourself that you are equipped to handle it? How will you move through the fear and keep moving forward?

Don't forget, you are focusing on the bigger goal: achieving something you have been dreaming about doing in your life and how that would feel when you get there. Focus on that great feeling you wish to experience and see if the fear subsides. Remember that taking action is one of the best antidotes to fear. By handling your fear in the moment, you are empowered to continue on your path to your best life chapter ever!

Using Progress as a Safety Net

When you are working toward making meaningful change that will disrupt your normal course of life, it is very comforting to know you have a plan to fall back on. It becomes your safety net. You can see the progress of your small steps in a visible way and you can use that progress to keep you moving forward toward your goal.

Here's an example of how this all comes together. Remember the story of Deb in Chapter 4? She worked for a large company, became part of their speakers' bureau and through that experience, realized her awesome potential. She had worked alongside other professionals and helped those professionals create their own personal wealth. She realized she could take the opportunity to shape her future and create her own wealth by starting her own business.

Her story is a great example of following this process because she identified her greatest desire, chose to pursue it, made her Next Life Chapter Declaration, and used that as the foundation for her planning process.

She took the steps to own her vision, not only by saying it out loud when she attended networking and training events, but by also sharing her vision with a few people who were very close to her.

Deb laid out her major milestones and created manageable, smaller steps that she got done on the weekends while working full time at the company. She created spreadsheets to manage her financial plan so she would know when the time was right to take the leap and quit her job. She kept taking action on her smaller steps to keep herself moving forward in achieving her next life chapter.

Deb told me it wasn't always easy, but she also said she wouldn't trade the experience of taking the leap and building her business for anything. She has had her business for 20 years now and has grown her customer base and her network of contacts and resources. She has over 40 associates that help her satisfy her clients' needs and has become very successful and involved in her community.

* * *

I hope you're now the proud owner of a Next Life Chapter Plan. If you are at that point, executing your plan will change your future. Many people who want to make meaningful change in their lives never get to the point of knowing the specific next step to take today to make it happen. You are now in control to create the life of your dreams. You have never been so prepared to make it happen. Congratulations!

Chapter 8 – The Value of Validation

"Internal validation is the most important."
Tina Meilleur

This step in the CRAVE™ process is the most important. Once you have started to take action on your plan, you actually have the opportunity to validate it. Let me explain what I mean by that. It's important to have an opportunity to tweak your plan or even start over and make a different choice about your dream. Some of the women I talked to who had started to make meaningful change in their life, had abandoned their plan because it didn't feel right for them. When they started taking action, what they'd chosen as a dream began to feel inauthentic or no longer like a good fit for them. At that point, they shut down and quit pursuing their dreams.

This step in the CRAVE™ process – "V" for "Validation" – is about being kind to yourself in the midst of continuing to pursue your dream. It's designed to allow you to hit the "pause" button, check in with yourself, and do a course correction, if necessary.

Instead of looking for external validation or approval about what you have chosen to pursue for your next life chapter, this step requires that you keep your focus on yourself. It's all about you (just like the rest of this process!). This step is your chance to make sure what you are pursuing feels right for you and keeps feeling right for you.

When I look up "validate" in the *Merriam-Webster Dictionary*, I find this definition: "to recognize, establish, or illustrate the worthiness or legitimacy of."

When you start to take action, identify how it feels. Does what you chose to take action on really demonstrate the legitimacy of your desire? You can also ask yourself these questions to check in and see if your plan is still valid for you:

- Does my next life chapter highlight my gifts and talents? If so, how? If not, what is missing?

- What about my next life chapter is starting to feel like a good fit for me?
- Why do I feel like I was meant to realize my next life chapter as I've designed it?
- When I started taking action to achieve my dream, what about it felt natural to me?

These questions can help you validate your plan internally. Rely on your intuition to help yourself really get in touch with how you feel. Using your intuition may not come naturally, but there are practical things you can do to increase that internal connection. That's what the next section is about.

Learning to Use Your Intuitive Wisdom

"The only real valuable thing is intuition."
Albert Einstein

Much of what I am asking you to do in this section is to buck your traditional culture and learn to rely on your intuitive wisdom. More than likely, you do experience your intuition, but quickly brush it aside. If you learned to follow it more often, your life would be more aligned with your heart's desire.

The key to learning to follow your intuitive wisdom is to develop the ability to "hear" or "feel" it. In order to do that, allow yourself to be quiet every once in a while and "tune in" to it. You may sense it or refer to it as instinct, a feeling in your gut, your inner voice, or a sixth sense.

This intuitive wisdom always knows what is true for you. That is why it is so important to get in touch with it. You can receive your validation internally by following your intuition. Then you will be able to tell if you are on the right path for your inner truth and what you are meant to do.

There are several steps you can take to "tune in" to your intuitive wisdom:

- **Learn to create quiet moments.** This will allow your intuition to come forward. You can learn to develop the ability to create those quiet moments. In those quiet moments you will be able to access your inner voice.

- **Practice noticing and quieting your inner critic.** Your inner critic – that other inner voice – is the inner voice that tells you why something you truly want won't work, why you don't deserve it, or that your goal isn't possible to achieve. The logical brain tends to put the brakes on new things we attempt to do, because it senses danger and simply wants to protect us. The logical brain can also take the form of your inner critic, offering many reasons why pursuing your dream is a bad idea. When you can identify that voice, you will be better able to distinguish between it and your intuition.

- **Journal to capture your thoughts and feelings.** Your journal entries can provide a window into your true feelings – the feelings that come up in your quietest moments. You can enjoy more success with this step if you create a habit to enter your thoughts into your journal when you are at your freshest and most open. Is this first thing in the morning for you? Or perhaps right before you go to sleep?

Inner Critic or Intuitive Wisdom?

As you've started to take action on your plan – or even if you haven't started yet, but have been thinking about it – what kinds of thoughts and feelings have been coming up for you? It's important to keep track of them, perhaps in your journal.

Confront each thought or feeling and identify the source of it. Is it because there is something society says you should be doing? Is it the voice of your mother? Is it a belief you have that it might be time to trade in your life for one that is a better fit for you? Refer to this list throughout the CRAVE™ process, as you continue to take steps, watch for opportunities, and validate your plan.

How do you tell if what you are feeling is your inner critic or your intuitive wisdom? When you are first learning to tell the difference, it can seem pretty difficult. If you are getting something from your inner critic that tells you "your plan is all wrong – you are going after the wrong thing," you might think it is your intuition giving you the message.

You can train yourself to react to such thoughts and feelings in a way that helps you sort it out. This involves understanding this sequence of cause and effect:

1. Your thoughts create your feelings.
2. Your feelings create your behaviors.
3. Your behaviors reinforce your thoughts.

This is a cycle you can learn to identify in order to rid yourself of the thoughts and behaviors that don't serve you. If you start to have a feeling or emotion that confuses you or feels really negative, try to peel back the emotion to get to the thought behind it. The more you do this, the easier it will be to notice and trust your intuition.

Here's an example of how to recognize this cycle. When I started preparing for my coaching career, I was really scared. I felt fear. However, I only recognized the feeling, not the thought behind it. When I felt that fear, I would become paralyzed and not take action in my business. When I stopped taking action in my business, I stopped moving forward and creating the business of my dreams. When I stopped moving forward, I wasn't successful. My resulting lack of success swirled around to fuel the thought that I had made the wrong decision to pursue my own coaching business.

Having a coaching business was my dream and I had a lot of my heart and soul invested in making it happen. How could I let fear get in the way? I was able to find a way to get beyond it and interrupt that cycle. Let me show you how to do this for yourself.

Maybe you're having doubts about what you are going to pursue for yourself. There are ways you can combat the fear and determine how to break through it. It begins with understanding what's underneath your fear. I'll break down a situation to show you how to get through that fearful episode and start moving forward again, and how the cycle can be interrupted and broken. Here is a possible sequence of steps for you to use to deconstruct what is happening and break the cycle so you can keep moving:

- When you recognize the emotion (like fear), ask yourself what is behind it.
- Identify the thoughts behind the fear. They can be something like this (and they may not be pretty):
  - "You won't be successful"

- o "What will your family/friends/former co-workers think?"
  - o "What makes you think you deserve to do something totally different and be successful?"
- Reframe the thoughts one by one by finding a counter-thought that feels better and is true for you:
  - o "I won't be successful" can turn into "I have been successful at everything I have put my heart and soul into, why would this be any different?"
  - o "What will my family/friends/former co-workers think?" can turn into "Why should I care what they think? If they truly care about me, they will be happy for me."
  - o "What makes me think I deserve to do something totally different and be successful in this new endeavor?" can turn into "I have great skills and experience and this new

152

endeavor is a great fit for my natural talents."

Call up evidence from your past to help you re-frame the emotion and the thoughts behind it, gathering evidence for the thoughts that are true for you and which feel better. That evidence can really take the wind out of the sails of those scary emotions. Those emotions can no longer survive in your head or your heart because you have no evidence to support their existence. Don't get me wrong, you aren't going to stop negative emotions from popping up in the future, and it is perfectly okay to allow yourself to feel them. Now you have the skills and tools to address them when they do get in your way. Your rational brain will try to protect you, but work in concert with it to logically provide evidence that your negative thoughts are not true.

It's Your Turn

Now that you have started to take action, is anything coming up for you that may get in the way of your dream? If so, let's begin to break those emotions down. Do a separate exercise for each emotion to bust through the ones that keep you from moving ahead.

I've provided a set of phrases here to get you started. Refer back to the example above if you get stuck.

1. When I prepared to take action on my Next Life Chapter Plan, I started to feel_____. (The feeling you identify in this step will be used to complete the rest of the exercise.)

2. My feeling of _____ is causing me to _____. (What is the feeling you identified in step 1 causing you to do? Stop, delay, question yourself?)

3. When I_____, I no longer _____. (What is the impact or outcome of what you are doing or not doing? Did you stop taking action altogether? Did you abandon your plan? Did you sabotage yourself?)

4. When I no longer _____, this is what happens: _____. (Identify the cascading impact of your emotions and behaviors.)

5. When this happens – _____ – then I assume I am making the wrong decision for

myself. (Identify the self-doubt associated with your actions.)

6. When I feel I am making the wrong decision for myself, I am filled with the emotions _____and _____. (Try to be clear about what emotions are coming up.)

Do you see how you can begin to pile more negative emotions on top of each other when you begin to doubt yourself?

Once you've written out an exercise about an emotion – about what you are feeling and how it is impacting you and your progress – you're ready to find evidence to show that the thoughts behind it are invalid. Feelings based on untrue thoughts don't feel any less real. This process is not about dismissing how you feel, but about using a tool to systematically and logically shift your thinking so you can move forward.

What's the Right Choice?

If you have processed your emotions and thoughts and you believe you have them under control, but you are still having problems moving forward, there is probably something else at play. At this point, you need to begin to examine whether your choice is just not the right one for you.

There are other ways to check in and determine if what you have chosen as your dream just isn't what you thought it might be. Here are some examples:

- A successful businesswoman dreams of the opportunity to open a retail store. This has been a lifelong dream, but when she starts to take action toward achieving her goal, she realizes how much time it will take before she makes a profit. Being profitable will afford her the flexibility to hire someone to take care of sales so she can do the things necessary to build the business. She is not sure she wants to be tied down to this lifestyle even for a few years.
- An introverted woman dreams of running a business in which she is a therapist and a healer. She realizes she would have the responsibility to market herself to get clients and this is not something she ever wanted to do. She simply wants to focus on serving the clients that someone else brings in.

- A successful law partner dreams of getting out of the rat race to go after his dream of working for a non-profit. Based on recent changes involving the declining health of his aging parents, he starts to feel the timing may not be right for exploring his dream.

It can be very helpful to determine whether the reasons you want to back away from your plan involve excuses, or whether your concerns are legitimate regarding why the choice you created a plan around is no longer right for you.

After you really take the time to review what you are feeling, and you've decided that the choice you have made in your declaration just isn't right for you or perhaps the timing isn't right, you can:

- go back through the process and make another choice – one that may be better suited for you at this time, or
- tweak the timeline for your milestones so you are working on your plan more slowly, to allow time for your legitimate constraints to get out of the way.

I don't advocate abandoning your dream, but maybe the dream you started out exploring isn't right for you anymore. For your next chapter, pursue a dream that's close to your heart. This might take a couple of tries to identify. The CRAVE™ process allows you to try things out and make adjustments and still wind up with a plan to follow.

Chapter 9 – What's a Journey Without Enjoying It Along the Way?

"Enjoyment is never overrated."
Tina Meilleur

The last step of the CRAVE™ process is "E" for "Enjoy." This step is about building more enjoyment and celebration into your everyday life. Your intention is to design your next chapter in a way that increases your enjoyment of life in general, but has you creating the habit of celebrating your wins more frequently. There should be joy every day in doing what you are meant to do in your life, and learning to enjoy what you have accomplished can be a way to practice and create new habits.

How Do You Build Enjoyment into Your Life?

"Your life isn't always measured by tangible results. What it really is in the end is the process, and what you learn about yourself and about life."
Vera Wang

The CRAVE™ process is your journey to plan and achieve your next life chapter. This is not always an easy journey, and it can be lonely. Your commitment to enjoying the journey is something you can do that will provide motivation when you start to feel stuck in your quest. Using this step of "enjoy," you will not only take the time to look back to see how far you have traveled on your path, but you will learn to find enjoyment along the way.

Enjoying what you do in life is one of the most important positive steps you can take toward achieving the success you desire. It makes you eager to get out of bed, makes your work not feel like work, and you have a better chance of removing obstacles that get in your way. When those around you see you enjoying your life or work, they are more eager to be around you and your positive energy. Your joy can be contagious, as are your achievements. Positive and successful people attract positive and successful people.

Enjoy Yourself Throughout the Process

Even though the "E" in CRAVE™ is for "Enjoy" and it's the last step in the process, it's meant to remind you to enjoy yourself *throughout* the CRAVE™ process. The art of finding enjoyment in the moment may not be one of your strongest skills. You may reserve your enjoyment for when you have time – and when is that? Enjoying yourself in the moment and taking time to celebrate accomplishments, big or small, are behaviors you can develop as new habits. New habits have a better chance of developing when they're planned for and reinforced.

You've already seen how you can lay the groundwork for making regular celebrations a new habit. In Chapter 7, you were invited to make a list of celebration items and allocate a celebration budget. That gives you things to choose from to celebrate, and the funds to make them happen. Celebration can become a new habit in no time at all!

You can also develop other sources of accomplishments to celebrate, besides that list from Chapter 7 (which you can keep updated). Hopefully, you have already gotten into the habit of taking notes throughout the process. Journaling can be used to capture all the things that may be worth celebrating. You can refer to your journal whenever you have a dip in your mood as well, or need some motivation.

More Celebration Increases Your Overall Enjoyment in Life

"I don't have to chase extraordinary moments to find happiness – it's right in front of me if I'm paying attention and practicing gratitude."
Brené Brown

In order to increase your overall enjoyment in your next life chapter, you should plan on adding more celebrations. I'm not referring to the traditional celebrations you may be used to, such as celebrating a family member's birthday, your wedding anniversary, your child's graduation, or your retirement. These are significant events in your life. Consider creating your own everyday celebrations, not because of a certain date on the calendar, and not relying on someone else to do it for you, but to honor the steps you take, the milestones you reach, and your progress toward your dream.

When you only celebrate special occasions, you tend to think you have to make them bigger and better each time, but I challenge you to experiment to see what kinds of celebration work best for you. Adding more celebration to your life in general, not only around your dream plan, will help you get into the spirit of looking for the good things in life and creating more enjoyment every day.

My husband and I have a standing joke about November being my "birthday month." He says there is no such thing, but I say there is if I say so! This is my way of spreading the enjoyment of my birthday over many more days. I don't expect a lavish gift, or a series of gifts, just because I want to celebrate my birthday over a month rather than on one day – that isn't the point. I use the month of November to remind me that I'm grateful to be here and in good health; I honor my father (who is no longer with us); I make sure to spend time with family and friends; and I spend some time on my actual birthday with my lovely and fun mom. Plus, the mention of the phrase, "It's my birthday month!" makes us laugh every time. As far as I'm concerned – mission accomplished!

How can you introduce more enjoyment into your life? Here's a start for you. If you have gone through any of the steps of the CRAVE™ process, there is already so much for you to enjoy and celebrate at this point, don't you think? Check in now to see what you can celebrate from going through this process:

- Have you chosen to put yourself first?
- Have you made your choice about what you would like to pursue for your next life chapter?
- Have you made your Next Life Chapter Declaration?
- Have you created your plan to achieve your most urgent desire?
- Have you begun taking action on your plan?
- Have you checked in with yourself to ensure you were headed in the right direction?

The fact you have engaged with any of those steps is a significant accomplishment and each step deserves to be enjoyed and celebrated!

Celebration Creates an Emotional Connection

"The more you praise and celebrate your life, the more there is in life to celebrate."
Oprah Winfrey

We're flooded with online information, social media, and the 24/7 news cycle in our daily lives. It can be easy to be swept away by the negativity embedded in all the challenges around the world and right in front of you. Some of the stories you hear may create an emotional connection and pull you into a negative space. You might not need to disconnect altogether, but sometimes it helps to recognize the need for balance regarding how you're investing your precious energy. Celebrating can help!

Celebrations, big or small, can create an emotional connection to your success and dispel negativity. Even the act of simply putting yourself first for a change is worthy of celebration. Celebrating the act of making yourself a priority will help you reinforce that behavior and, before long, it will be easier to focus on continuing to do something for yourself. The more you make yourself a priority, the more those around you will realize how important you are to yourself. They will more than likely move toward helping you get the space and support you need.

Let's not confuse celebration with recognition. Recognition is something you do, or is done to you, but celebration is something you feel. As an example, when you get your college degree, you walk across the stage to receive your diploma. That is recognition. Having a party before or after you receive your diploma, alone or with family and friends – now that's celebration! Celebration is a personal, emotional connection to your achievement. The receipt of the diploma is a formality; the party is something you feel in your heart and soul.

Here's an example of a different type of celebration, one that remains in my heart. It involves my city of New Orleans and is very personal to me. In post-Hurricane Katrina New Orleans (2005), the New Orleans Saints, the city's NFL football team, took on an almost symbolic role in the return of the city to normalcy. The first game the Saints played in the previously damaged Superdome was an emotionally charged day, but the years that followed gave us an even bigger celebration.

When the New Orleans Saints won the Super Bowl in 2009, the team received the Super Bowl trophy as recognition of their achievement. However, the celebration became much stronger and more heartfelt. Within a couple of weeks, there was a huge parade in the City of New Orleans, complete with Mardi Gras floats, marching bands, and the New Orleans Saints players and coaches. This celebration was the emotional connection the city's residents had to this win – it was amazing! For me, I celebrated and felt the emotion of that day deep in my heart.

How to Make Celebration a Priority

In the normal course of a day or a month, particularly when you get busy, time for self-care and celebrations may be the first things to go. Just like I scheduled social times on my calendar to get myself out of my home office, you can schedule appointments with and for yourself for celebration. The key is not only to schedule the time, but to actually do what you have on your schedule! If one of your celebrations is to get a massage, make the appointment and then keep it. If one of your celebrations is to have a golf game with a group, set it up and then actually show up for your tee time. This is something you can control. Don't consider cancellation an option unless there is a critical reason for it. Share your plans with others so they can help you stay accountable.

I hope I have convinced you how important it is to add the element of celebration to your Next Chapter plan and follow through. Practice regularly so you create a new habit of celebration that becomes automatic. This habit of celebration can only add to your enjoyment of your new life chapter.

Chapter 10 – Inside the CRAVE™ Process and What You Can Expect

"Breaking through barriers is the way we make room for meaningful change."
Tina Meilleur

This chapter is dedicated to helping you identify the barriers you may run into as you go through the CRAVE™ process. You can quickly refer to this chapter when you run into a challenge or an opportunity. Then you can say "Aha! This is normal." When something is expected, you don't have to stop and spend your energy trying to figure it out.

Being prepared and proactive is key in dealing with these barriers, and this chapter can help with that. If you think any of the themes I listed below have any truth for you, being prepared to deal with both the situation and the people involved will help you stay on track to your dream.

I've organized these examples around five major themes, to make them easier to find when you need them:

1. Fear of failure
2. Your change is their change
3. Fear of success
4. Adapting to your new identity
5. Shaping your destiny

You may identify with some of these themes and not with others, but none of them are barriers that are insurmountable. Your wins and your ability to work through whatever barriers pop up for you as you create your next chapter are to be celebrated.

Fear of Failure

"Success is often achieved by those who don't know that failure is inevitable."
Coco Chanel

Fear of failure is a big concern for many of my clients. I know it was for me. I love the quote above by Coco Chanel because it speaks to not letting fear of failure get in your way. If you don't believe you can fail, you will keep moving. If you learn from your "failures," does it count as a failure? You will never know what you are capable of until you try. If you allow the fear of failing at something new to get in the way, you may never attempt to achieve your biggest dreams.

Many of my clients see their fear of failure as the biggest obstacle in their way. But we never really know if we'll fail or succeed until we try. Taking action is the single best way to face your fears. Have you heard of Broadway performers who get sick right before they go out on stage – almost paralyzed by stage fright? They make themselves sick over their fear of failing in their performance – not getting their lines right, or missing a mark. The beautiful thing is that they go out on stage anyway. And what if they make a mistake? If they're dedicated to what they're doing, they'll learn from their mistake and that will make their next performance that much better.

It may be natural for you to have a fear of failure, but it becomes a dangerous threat to your dream *when you allow it to keep you from doing the things you love*. Life is about taking chances. Failure may be part of what happens when you take a chance.

The key to recovering from failures, large or small, is to learn what the failures have to teach you and then adjust your plan based on that learning.

Your Change Is Their Change

"Don't let the noise of others' opinions drown out your own inner voice."
Steve Jobs

Many of my clients have run into the issue of how their own changes prompt others around them to change. When they shared their plans to make big changes in their life, they began to understand how their friends and family would also be affected. When you begin to make big life changes, or even announce your intention to do so, those closest to you may see your major change as a threat to what they know and experience about you. They have a certain relationship with you that is dependable and maybe even predictable, and they're afraid that relationship will change.

Some of those closest to you simply want to protect you. It may appear they are not supportive, however, they come from a place of caring and love for you. They have either been where you are and want to warn you about the pitfalls, or they don't want to see you suffer if what you are going after may not work out.

How do you deal with the emotions of those around you as you change? View their concerns from their point of view and try to determine why they're concerned. Is it because:

- they are worried about the fate of their relationship with you and how it will change when you change?
- they don't want you to be hurt if something doesn't work out for you?
- they interpret your need to change as a sign that they need to change as well?
- they worry that your current state is no longer good enough for you and they may not be good enough to participate in the world of the "new you"?

If you pay attention to the concerns they raise, talk to them, ask questions, and listen to their responses, you will be better prepared to understand their reactions and underlying emotions. That will help you determine how to communicate why you are making the changes you have planned.

Communication is the key to quelling their fears. And if you can't quell their fears, you may need to go ahead and make the changes you need to anyway.

Fear of Success

"We know what we are, but know not what we may be."
William Shakespeare

The fear of success can mask itself in many ways. If you have a fear of success, you may worry about losing what is familiar, and that can cause you to come to a complete stop in taking action on your goals. You may even experience feelings of not being worthy of success. Even though it may be a challenge to uncover what's beneath your lack of action, it could be a fear of success that's having a paralyzing effect on you.

Maybe you're committed to making change, have a plan that you fully support, and start taking action, but then all of a sudden you get to a particular step and, before you can execute it, you stop cold. Maybe you're interpreting that particular step as *the* step that will get you closer to your goal and cause you to lose what is familiar to you. If a step in your plan appears to be a turning point, after which you will be too far along to reverse things or change direction easily, it may become a signal for you to pause or stop. You may begin to ask yourself questions like these:

- "Will I be able to meet the expectations I have of myself in my next life chapter?"
- "Will I lose too much of what is familiar and safe?"
- "Will there be additional demands made on me that I can't yet see and won't like?"

Ask the questions, but keep validating your plan and taking steps, because a turning point also means that your goal is in sight! Remember that.

If your fear of success is caused by a feeling that you are not worthy of the success you are pursuing, the expectations you've attached to achieving your goal may be what is stopping you. You can begin to sort this out by asking yourself if your fear of success is a signal that you're actually getting closer and closer to your goal, so the success is right around the corner. What thoughts can you examine to find evidence that you deserve every bit of success you are close to achieving? You may begin to ask yourself questions like these:

- "Why do I not feel worthy to accept the success that may be around the corner for me?"
- "What is coming up for me as I am getting closer to achieving my goal?"
- "What expectations am I attaching to this potential level of success for myself?"

Remember that you are working to create a future around your most special gifts and talents and you're moving toward doing things that really align with your life's purpose. Don't let your fear of success get in the way of what you truly want and absolutely deserve. Take your emotions and examine them, break them down, and move on.

Adapting to Your New Identity

"To be yourself in a world that is constantly trying to make you something else is the greatest accomplishment."
Ralph Waldo Emerson

Particularly if the changes you are making in your life involve moving from one career to another or significantly changing the focus of your life, there are likely to be challenges as you adapt to your new identity. As I transitioned from my corporate role to my new role as an entrepreneur, it took me a great deal of time to get comfortable and own that new identity.

Achieving your next life chapter may give you a whole new identity, one that's much more true to you. If you change careers, like I did, you will need to get comfortable communicating in the language of your new identity. This is why I invited you to create a Next Life Chapter Declaration as your statement of what you chose to pursue during this process. You may need to tweak it a bit to keep it current, but stating your declaration out loud can help you with making the adaptation to your new identity.

Even if you aren't making major life changes like a change in career, but are focusing more on the balance you need in your life, you, too, may need to adapt to a new identity. As an example, if you were always the "go-to" person for volunteering, but have decided to back off to ensure you have more time for yourself, your new identity may include saying "no" more often.

In either example above, the key to adapting successfully is to own your new identity – step into it as fully as you can and in as many ways as you can. This will take some work. You can practice articulating your new identity by identifying with your new identity in your speech or actions, or by making a written announcement to help you with ownership of your new identity.

Another exercise is to recall a bad day in your life before you starting taking action. If you were unhappy or unfulfilled, think back about how that felt and compare that to the feelings you connect to when you imagine stepping into your next chapter and realizing the dream you're working toward. This thought process can be a big motivator for owning your new identity!

Shaping Your Destiny

"Surround yourself with people who are smarter than you. Pick people who are interested in what you're interested in."
Russell Simmons

This challenge is about issues that can arise when you move toward surrounding yourself with like-minded people – your tribe! As you go through your plan to achieve your next life chapter, there will be people around you who just won't get what you're doing. They won't understand what you're after, or why you want things to change. They'll question whether you will be able to pull off getting to your goal. In these cases, you have to stay focused and you can't worry about their opinions. Create some distance between you and those who don't understand where you are headed and why.

Others may wallow in their own self-pity or lack of accomplishment when they hear about what you're doing. They may make excuses about why they can't be successful, using phrases like "if only," "when I can," etc. Just like the people who won't understand what you are doing, those who wallow in their own shortcomings are also people to create some distance from.

Surround yourself with people who are really vested in your success and don't pull you down into their drama. They will help you keep your energy flowing in the direction of reaching your goals. Remember, you are executing a plan to fulfill your most urgent desire in life. Why allow anyone or anything to get in your way?

Creating distance from people who don't offer the proper support may be difficult to do, but it's really necessary. People who can't accept the changes you are making may not understand the changes or may be jealous you're taking action and they are not. Be bold in asking for what you need. If those around you cannot provide that environment for you, they are not people who should be sharing in the achievement of your goals.

Success breeds success. If you surround yourself with "can-do" people and people who are already successful or are well on their way, you will feel motivated when you're in their presence.

* * *

Creating the proper environment to shape your new destiny is the best thing you can do for yourself. Take some time to determine what needs to be in place so you can feel supported and motivated to achieve what you truly want. You should match the importance of the environment and support you need to the intensity of your desire to achieve what you are going after. When there is alignment of these two things, you will be unstoppable.

Chapter 11 – Wrapping It All Up

This chapter is all about wrapping up the topics we discussed and sending you on your way with confidence and commitment so you are well prepared and remain on the right track as you create your dream.

What About Being Vulnerable?

It is your willingness to go to that place of vulnerability that will enable you to uncover your deepest, most urgent desire and get to your place of truth. I hope by now you feel you have a safe place in which to be vulnerable and explore your deepest needs and wants for your future.

As you allow yourself to experience your vulnerability, you will see how much freedom it gives you to explore what you truly want. Once you start to have that experience, you will understand why being in that state is so valuable for you. There is no substitute for letting go and participating fully in the process of redesigning your life.

Years ago, I wanted to learn how to paint in watercolors. I'm no artist, but I love the way watercolor paintings invite me in, because they seem soft and less than perfect. I decided to take a class and learn some watercolor painting techniques. I didn't take a drawing class first, but decided to be vulnerable and just show up. I went every week and I practiced the techniques taught by my teacher, an accomplished multi-media artist. I had a lot of fun. Whenever I thought I had made a mistake, my teacher would say, "Oh, you've had a happy accident. Look at the effect you got there." Even when we showed our work to our fellow students at the end of each class, and I saw that many of the other students were very skilled artists, I would celebrate my happy accidents and the fact that I had allowed myself to be vulnerable and open. I'd taken the class to have an experience, and it turned into one that would expand my horizons. I have never forgotten that "happy accident" phrase.

One of my friends asked me why I decided to take that class. I thought for a moment and said, "Anything I have ever wanted to do that doesn't come naturally, I have had to learn. I assumed watercolor painting was no different." Learning watercolor painting – or designing your next life chapter – both require making a decision to start, finding support and a teacher or mentor (someone who has been there and can guide you), committing to taking action and being vulnerable, and sticking with it to see what happens.

Throughout the CRAVE™ process, it helps so much to be willing to expand your own horizons. Get immersed in the experience and take action, so that you have your own "happy accidents." When you are on the road to designing your next life chapter, you will experience many twists and turns that are not in your plan. Each of those diversions will be an opportunity to explore what they have to teach you and in what direction they can take you. They are not meant to take you off course, but to show you opportunities you haven't yet envisioned for yourself.

It is not until you begin your journey and open yourself up to the possibilities the journey has to offer that you will be able to craft the best version of your future.

Selectively Leaving Your Past Behind

"When you know better, [you] do better."
Maya Angelou

The same past that makes you who you are can keep you from realizing your most brilliant future. The experiences of your past have shaped you into the person you have become and are valuable pieces of your persona. The wisdom you have developed can propel you into making great decisions about your life's best options, even if you choose to leave the hurt behind.

You have probably had some experiences that did not work out very well for you, but you can harvest the learning from those experiences so that what you learned can become part of crafting your plan for your next life chapter.

Use your experiences as fuel for finding what is most true in your heart. If you consider the times when you felt really dejected, those memories can really inform what you need from your future in order to feel more fulfilled. This will require you to get quiet and dive into your thoughts and memories and remember how you felt during those times of intensity. It can be challenging. You might begin by setting an intention such as, "I would like to understand which experiences from my past can offer me the wisdom to inform my decisions in creating my ideal next life chapter."

What you capture about those experiences can offer you specific input about what you would like and what you would not like to repeat as experiences. That's your goal. It's important to try to understand what about those experiences didn't work and why. Remember that if you take some of the same actions, you will likely get the same results. Finding the lessons from your experiences can help you get results that will be more aligned with where you want to go.

Let go of "could have" and "should have" – those phrases can keep you stuck. Instead of saying things like, "If this had happened, I could have _____," or "I should have _____ when I had the chance, but it's too late now," eliminate those phrases from your vocabulary.

Be willing to find the lessons and move on. This can be a powerful action for you.

Breaking Down Overwhelm

I know I've given you lots to think about in undertaking this project for yourself and I know it can be overwhelming. In writing this book, I've done what I've asked you to do – break the big steps down into smaller ones to help control the overwhelm.

You may get stuck as you work through the steps of the CRAVE™ process. That's natural and part of why you may feel overwhelmed at times. You may begin to question why you even started this effort. You may move between excitement and fear. You may think this isn't the right time for you to do this. The beauty of this process is that you can make a plan and put your own timeline to it.

Think about the example of building a new house. You don't just dream of a house and then it appears. It happens because you put a plan together and take steps to set aside funds, decide where you want your house to be located, how it should function for you, and what you need the house to look like. You have architectural drawings made and a construction plan in place for what needs to happen every week and month of the building process. This allows you to plan and have an estimate of the date when you can move into your house.

Treat your next life chapter the same way: Take time to make some decisions and put a plan in place. You will not only be happy you did; you will set yourself up to succeed.

That's why it's so important to choose to put yourself first. Even with a plan, you don't know if your life will unfold exactly as you have laid it out. It rarely does. When your plan is based solidly on you, you have access to the clarity of direction needed to keep moving forward. You can also recognize the changes that can surface and the opportunities that will propel you closer to where you want to be.

The Power of Your Words

The purpose of the Your Next Life Chapter Declaration exercise is to give you a strong foundation and a starting point for owning your next life chapter. When you have this, you can really begin to believe in what is possible for you and you come to recognize the power of your words. In this way, you will increasingly own the vision of your new life and how you will feel when it becomes a reality.

It wasn't until I began to own my vision for my new career as a life and business coach that the vision became possible. I went through coach training, but that didn't get me there. I also learned new business tools for this new career, but it wasn't until I began to articulate how my life would be after achieving my goal that it finally started to become a reality.

In your journey to create your next life chapter, you will be challenged to break through the negative thoughts that threaten to influence your belief in yourself. You may question whether you are on the right path and whether you are taking the right steps. The words you use with yourself and others will be extremely important as you go through this process. Your words are a reflection of what you want and where you want to go.

When you refer to your next life chapter, instead of starting your sentences with, "I want to...," try saying, "I will...!" This slight adjustment will give you so much power and strengthen your attitude and your belief that your dream will become a reality.

You Are Worth It

The best way to get what you really want out of life is to determine what you really need. Get very clear on this, since it will shape your future. You may have spent much of your life settling for things or situations that were less than perfect for you. I'm not necessarily talking about the surface complaints you might have about your job or your relationships. I'm talking about the deep needs you have that should be deal-breakers for you. These may be the needs you have put on the back burner, or have even denied being aware of, but if you are going to design a new life chapter for yourself, don't you feel your deepest needs should be met? If not, why would you bother to make changes and cause disruption for yourself if, in the end, you would simply be left with those same deep needs unmet?

My message to you is that you are worth it. You are worth every effort you make to get what you truly need in your life.

I was in a Suzanne Evans workshop this past year and she had us do an exercise to identify what we had been tolerating in our lives. This was a powerful exercise, because it helped me identify the things I'd let slide, even though they bothered me terribly. I realized that the more I tolerated, the less I honored my real needs and wants. Think about ways you settle for less and how that relates to not getting your most urgent needs met.

Earlier in the book, you identified your personal core values. In designing your next life chapter, you will ensure that those values are integrated into what you create. Stay focused on your personal core values. Do not settle for things that are incongruent with what you need in your life to stay emotionally healthy. Don't lose sight of your own life priorities.

Where are you settling? This is an important concept for you to return to. It will help you unlock what holds you back from taking action. Where you are willing to settle is exactly where you won't be as aligned with your true wants and needs.

Believe Your Life Can Be Better Now

When you have your plan in place and start taking action, your life will start to change. Even as you begin to create your plan, but before you start to take action on it, you may start to feel differently about your present life.

You don't need to wait to start feeling differently. Here are some ways you can create a truer and more aligned life, even as you work out your Next Chapter plan:

- Practice saying "no" to things that don't feel right for you.
- Address something on your list of things you are tolerating in your life.
- Share your dreams with someone close to you.
- Shift your energy to a positive space when you start to feel overwhelmed.
- Forgive yourself when you don't get everything done.
- Accept that you can delegate some tasks to get them off your plate.
- Schedule time for your own self-care.
- Find time to "check out" in order to get quiet time.
- Ask for what you need from those who love and care for you.

Don't wait. The sooner you focus on yourself, the sooner you will start seeing results. If you look back on what you have documented already as you've gone through any of the steps of the CRAVE™ process, you will see plenty of opportunities for taking small steps that will help you feel better about yourself and where you are headed.

I Am So Proud of You

Celebrate the beginning of your journey, which you've completed just by reading this book! I wrote it with you in mind and I am so proud of you for recognizing your need for guidance on the topic of achieving your dreams. If my pride in you could propel you to reach your most urgent desires for your life, you would already be there! That's how proud I am of you!

The first step required to making significant change is recognizing and acknowledging your desire to make those changes. It's also important to understand your reason for change – your "why." Whatever brought you here, I'm very proud of you for getting to this point in your journey.

I also recognize how special you are. There are so many people who wish to create their own next life chapter. What makes you special is that you are willing to do what it takes to make it happen. In a little while, as you tune in to yourself and your dreams and go through the steps of the CRAVE™ process, you will be able to look back to where you started and see how far you have come. You will be celebrating!

I believe you are courageous, committed, positive, caring, genuine, brave, unselfish, and motivated. Those qualities will carry you through as you continue your journey of designing your next life chapter – for yourself, as only you can. And remember, I am here for you if you run into trouble or want support.

If you haven't already, now would be a good time to take your complimentary quiz to see how you are doing in living your ideal life so far. You can sign in to access it at: www.yourideallifequiz.com.

And remember to retake the quiz again when you finish the process and have started living your next life chapter, so you can compare that end result to the first time you took the assessment. Comparing your new score to your original score will show you how much progress you've made.

In Closing

The journey for each and every one of you to create your next life chapter will be unique. Each of you may follow a different path, on a different timeline, to reach a different future state meant just for you. What will remain consistent is the dedication and commitment it will take to make your dreams a reality.

I created the CRAVE™ process because I knew that as you got comfortable in your own life and what you had accomplished, it would be extremely difficult to undertake the actions needed in order to make meaningful change in your life.

I knew because it happened to me. I was too comfortable to voluntarily bring disruption into my life. It would have been far easier to make the choice to go back into the familiar and get another corporate job after my layoff. By following my own process, I was able to dig deep and uncover my life's calling and what would bring me joy.

I wanted to lead you by the hand and tell you everything would be okay. I wanted to warn you about what you could expect and give you the tools to keep going. I wish I'd had someone to help me navigate my own journey, but I didn't, so I want to share what I learned by trial and error. I also wanted you to benefit from my experience with my clients – where they got stuck and how we got past those issues.

I also wanted you to know that it's never too late. You have so much to offer and you may not realize it. Nothing you have ever done in your life is wasted. Find the lessons in your experiences, both positive and negative, and learn to use those lessons to your advantage.

Making change is not always easy, but because you have already taken the step of reading this book, you are much further along the path than most. Keep that momentum going!

I have learned to live my life consistent with what I wrote in this book and I want you to enjoy that freedom as well. It is with that intention that I send you on your way, with a virtual hug and a push to go ahead and start enjoying the positive energy of your next chapter as soon as possible. You only have one life to live and it should be the best it can be!

Acknowledgments

As I was growing up, writing a book and speaking in front of people were probably the most unlikely things I ever thought I would do. But, here I am, now a published author, a life and business coach, and a public speaker. This is a testament to the power of my parents allowing me to believe anything was possible for me.

My father worked in a blue-collar job all his life. He lived with the physical effects of having endured polio as a child. He illustrated strength and love each day as he worked hard to give us a better life than he had. My mother went back to work to help fund the family needs and provide a private-school education for me and my sister. She was a pillar of strength in the way she combined her career with managing our family. Our parents loved us and wanted to give us the best they could afford, even in the midst of their own sacrifices.

They both taught me to appreciate my gifts and talents and to believe that anything I could dream about was possible. They never discouraged me, although they did have the expectation that I would always do my best. They allowed me to learn how to take more risks than they did, all while in the safe environment of our childhood home. My mom is still a constant source of laughter and support in my life and I love her dearly.

I've had great mentors and bosses, people who recognized my talents and allowed me to fly higher than I'd thought I could. They allowed me to stretch, make mistakes, and learn more than I could have from any book.

My dear sister, my extended family, and my true friends have always been there for me. They pick me up when I am down, they celebrate my wins with me, and they are always available for advice. They have been an invaluable part of my support system. I love them all!

My dear husband and my stepson have been the center of my life for the last 15 years. I feel loved and supported every day. They are my touchstone, and fuel my desire to be successful. I could not ask for a more supportive life partner than my husband. In acknowledging my family, I must mention my chocolate lab, Roxie, who is my work companion and often my muse. Her unconditional love and her desire to play are lessons for me every day.

About the Author

Tina Meilleur is a life and business coach, author, speaker, the founder of Design Your Success. Her mission is to help high achievers match their skills with the opportunities they wish to create for themselves. Her "Next Chapter" program and CRAVE™ process are systematic approaches that can be used for making simple "tweaks" or orchestrating a total reinvention. She works with people all across the US and in international locations.

In her life and business coaching, Tina helps her clients in several ways:

- Working with those who are motivated to create a life that is more satisfying and rewarding and provide them with flexibility and confidence.
- Helping high-achieving female leaders bring the power of their Feminine Impact™ to the forefront of their leadership.
- Assisting female entrepreneurs with focus on flexibility and profitability in their businesses to bring their businesses to the next level.
- Conducting exclusive Mastermind groups that provide valuable business coaching for those who want to dig in to find ways to grow their businesses in profitable ways.
- Providing business consulting services that help teams and/or processes run more smoothly.

Tina has a CPA designation in the State of Louisiana and received her MBA from Tulane University in their Executive MBA program. She worked in small business and in a Fortune 500 company prior to starting her own business. Her experience areas include executive coaching, mentoring leaders, human resources, supply chain, operations management, project management, and budgeting. Because of her education and experience, Tina is a highly sought-after mentor, coach, facilitator, and speaker.

She lives in New Orleans, Louisiana, with her husband and stepson and a chocolate lab, Roxie. She fills her life with inspiration from writing, art, music, and being of service to others.

Thank You

I extend a heartfelt thank-you to you for taking the time to read this book. Writing it was a labor of love to you, and I am so honored to have you as one of my readers.

Do you have any unanswered questions? I invite you to reach out to me to ask questions and to keep me posted on your progress. I genuinely want to hear how you are doing and what you are able to accomplish!

With each revelation you experience, trust yourself in the process and remember that if what you chose to focus on truly doesn't feel right, you can go through the process again and choose another one of your desires to focus on. Dead ends are dealt with in the CRAVE™ process, so don't worry – just revisit the process until you've chosen a different focus that feels better.

Again, here are the links I provided:

- **Ideal Life Quiz.** If you haven't taken advantage of the initial assessment yet to get a baseline of where you are today in living your ideal life, you can find it at this address www.yourideallifequiz.com to sign up and take it now. You can take it again when you've started living your dream life, to compare the two and see your progress!

- **Your Next Chapter Facebook Group.** You have the opportunity to interact with other interested readers of this book in the Your Next Chapter Facebook Group, a secret Facebook group only for people who have the link from the book. It is designed to be a safe community for interacting, sharing your experiences, and getting support. You can join the closed Facebook group by searching for: "Your Next Chapter Book Group".

Please feel free to reach out to me if this book has piqued your interest and you would like to learn more about my other programs: group coaching, online courses, exclusive VIP coaching and retreats. Feel free to reach out to us for information: wecare@designyoursuccess.com.

If you need help understanding how you can move forward, you may qualify for a complimentary strategy session. Take advantage of the Ideal Life Quiz assessment above to see if you qualify for a 45-minute session with me to discuss your next steps. Thanks again and I wish you a successful journey!

58295168R00114

Made in the USA
Charleston, SC
08 July 2016